Breaking Golf's Last Barrier

Tracy A Reed

Dedication

To my wife Mary, who has supported my journey through the many ups and downs. I couldn't have finished this without her.

Acknowledgements

I would like to acknowledge all of the golfers who have participated in any of my programs over the years. Your questions and feedback have ultimately brought me to write this book. I was answering an email and this inspirational thought popped out of my head. As soon as I wrote it, I knew it had to be in the book:

The secret to both life and golf is balance, so one just needs to master balance...

Introduction

As I stood on the 16th tee box watching my shot, one thought nagged me as it had for the past 5 years. When moments ago I was contending for the lead, suddenly winning was no longer the goal. As I watched my provisional shot head out of bounds near my first shot, I knew this familiar scene would continue to repeat itself until I found the real answers I was seeking.

I had read everything in print on golf and watched nearly every video, but no answer. I practiced until my fingers bled, with no change in this circumstance. I could hit any shot with any club on command, but somehow I couldn't stop my game from blowing up somewhere during the round. When I watched the top PGA players on TV, I knew an answer existed, and I was going to find it if it took the rest of my life.

"How do they play golf week in and week out without a complete breakdown in their game along the way?"

I knew too many very good golfers whose games also broke down for no obvious reason, usually when they were playing their best rounds. I would never be able to enjoy golf until I answered that one question.

I found the answers and although they aren't complicated…

My quest to find my answers took over 25 years.

What I found is a mix of the simplification of the golf swing and a real understanding of the form and function of the mind in golf. This book will share all of that with you in an attempt to free you from the confusion that the game of golf seems to carry with it.

Where to start…

The roots of golf are sketchy at best. I can imagine a shepherd in a field in Scotland contemplating his life; he picks up a stick or maybe turns his crook around and whacks a rock… And it feels good.

Later he shows one of his friends this new trick and it soon becomes a competition to see who can hit a rock farther. You can see where this goes.

My point is that the game of Golf very well could have started with a man contemplating his life. I believe golf parallels life in many ways. In life, success starts with knowing yourself. In golf, success starts with understanding your inner workings and how to control your mind and body.

In golf and in life these two points are complicated by distractions. In life you're distracted by TV, radio, video games, your phone, your job and so on. In golf, the distractions are the target, the ball and the swing.

Once that shepherd and his friends started hitting rocks with sticks more, they may have started looking for the best rocks to hit, and then better sticks to hit them with. In the winter hitting those rocks stung their hands so they started carving wood into balls and later stuffing stitched leather balls with feathers. What started as an inner reflection on life quickly became distracted by the activity.

Today, more than ever, golf is a game of distractions. The hole, the ball, the club and the swing are all distractions because no matter how much better you make any of them, you won't succeed until you learn how to control your mind and body.

You may think, "Whoa, the golf swing is a distraction?"

Yes, the golf swing is something we try to make happen around the outside of our body, but in fact, the swing is created by inner body movement, which is created first in the mind. All of the new fangled golf instruction you've seen in the last ten years is actually a distraction to the real keys for success in golf because the instruction is focused on WHAT the body does during a golf swing (a result) rather than HOW the body does it (the cause).

The mainstream mental coaching is also a distraction to the golfer looking to succeed because it is focused on your thoughts which are a <u>result</u> of the mental process just as the swing is a <u>result</u> of an inner mental/physical process.

As golfers, we all are looking to improve our results, but to do so, <u>we must address the process that yields the results</u>.

But first, you must know HOW the process works and WHY it works. <u>Without the how and why, you will not remember the fix</u>, which means you will repeat those same mistakes until you get to the root cause. It doesn't make sense to pay an instructor to constantly point out the same mistakes or worse, to try fixing your golf swing with instruction that causes new problems.

My goal is to give you all of the information to completely understand the real processes behind the golf swing so that you have the tools to stay on track without the false hope that accompanies standard golf lessons. I was there too and I know the agony all too well.

I started this journey into the inner workings of golf in my mid 20's. After snatching defeat from the jaws of victory too many times, I realized that this game would be a tough nut to crack. I did what many other golfers do when challenged; I decided to learn everything I could about the game. After a few years of struggle, lots of golf lessons from highly rated instructors, and only average improvement, something terrible happened. I injured my back. I didn't just strain it, I messed it up so bad that I couldn't finish a round of golf because my leg would go numb.

I refused to give in to the injury because I was hooked on the game. I researched for ways to play golf without hurting my back further and how to play with little to no practice. My research eventually led me into biomechanics, which allowed me to complete at least the full round when I did play, but I was still limited to one round every two weeks if I wanted to function afterward. It didn't matter that my injury was limiting me, I still wanted more. I wanted to play well, and play well consistently. (I don't ask for much, do I?)

During my search it became evident that the golf instruction available to golfers was flawed and that some of those flaws were leading to the aggravation of my injury. I owned about 20 years of golf magazines and started seeing patterns in how their articles were written. I realized that modern golf instruction didn't solve problems, but rather replaced them with different ones. Over the span of 20 years, the same articles would resurface every few years, written differently, but usually with the same tips and conclusions that often led to other problems. When I discovered this well hidden hoax, I was really fired up.

I decided to figure out what was missing and make sure it was available to golfers who wanted to improve the way I wanted to improve. My journey took much longer than I had anticipated. It took 15 years to find a method where the average golfer could become above average rather quickly and now 30 years into this journey, I can say I finally cracked the nut that is golf.

In 2000, I wrote Golf Swing Control after about 15 years of research, testing, and 3 years sharing the information with over 5000 golfers around the world. The Golf Swing Control Manual shows golfers how to improve, gain consistency, and cut back on practice. I thought I had golf figured out. The manual is still a great resource for the average golfer looking to improve their game without needing constant lessons.

Looking back, I realize I made a few mistakes with Golf Swing Control, but overall, the area where I am questioned most turns out was not a mistake. When I wrote the manual, I didn't create any videos to go with it. They didn't come along until another company convinced me videos were needed.

It turns out that I had more golfers who "didn't get it" after the videos than before the videos were produced. The videos were produced to support the manual, but not replace it and unfortunately, too many golfers never read the manual once they had the videos.

To test, I went back to using the manual without the videos and again, golfers "get it" much better without video.

You might ask why the videos hurt golfers' progress. I believe it takes away the imagination that stimulates internal visualization. I wrote the manual in a way to promote visualization, which is then carried to the process of the golf shot. I believe that while video gives golfers a visual experience to try to copy, it doesn't connect them internally with the feelings that accompany that experience. Those feelings are where true and free control of movement is found.

My goal in Golf Swing Control was to give golfers a way to monitor and control their golf swings on the golf course; something that had never been done. Mission accomplished... Or so I thought.

My better golfers needed more for competition because their minds were getting in the way. I did some more research and applied some secrets from my days as an Army Interrogator to Golf Swing Control and discovered a hidden visual component of the golf swing that not only increased accuracy, but also kept the conscious mind quiet during the golf swing. I called this process Bio-Visual Focus and I thought nothing would top it.

I was so amazed at the results I was seeing with Bio-Visual Focus, I wanted to share it with my colleagues around the world.

A funny thing happened. Golf swing instructors told me that what I was doing was impossible. Mental coaches also told me that I was nuts, but the results told the real story.

All this time, I had no idea that I wasn't supposed to discover these breakthroughs, but I did, and the rest of the world treated me like they treated Columbus when he declared that the world is round. The results my students get have more than proven that my methods are entirely sound.

There was still one last barrier to break through. I kept seeing it every week on TV and reliving past personal experiences every time I saw it. The last barrier is that sudden unexplained breakdown of your golf game somewhere during a round. Bio-Visual Focus was close to fixing it, but there had to be a few additions.

This book is the first step toward breaking down golf's last barrier. I say that because you will need to read, apply and review this information regularly until you know you have broken the barrier.

This last barrier is a tough one to break. It requires a command of both your conscious and subconscious minds plus full awareness of the small changes in your golf game. Each change becomes a trigger for certain routines to right the ship. The hardest parts are building awareness and having the instinct to use the routines.

As in all of my training, this book brings together body and mind in a unified approach that puts you in total harmony with your golf game.

Enjoy the book and contact me if you have questions or wish to pursue further training.

How to Apply This Instruction to your Golf Game

First and foremost, I would like you to read through the whole book before applying any of this information. I know that will be a monumental task because you will be tempted many times along the way to pick up a club and try all of this out...

I completely understand.

I asked golfers to do the same thing with Golf Swing Control as well. Some did and many didn't. I only ask you to read through once first so that you have the big picture and you will know how each piece fits. Golfers who did this using Golf Swing Control had better and faster results than the golfers who just couldn't hold back. Believe me I'm one of those who have a hard time holding back, so either way, you'll be ok.

Golfers ask me what mistakes I correct the most. It's a good question, and the answer may surprise you. Years ago, I gave a seminar for 20 members where we videotaped their swings and I critiqued them on the spot. Afterward, I went through the videos with the intention of giving further advice based on slowing down the video and examining their swing more in detail. This process was very labor intensive, taking about 3 hours per video. After the first few videos, I stopped recording my critiques and made faster reviews of the rest.

In every single case, the swing problems were created by some shortcut the golfer had taken during the setup routine!

The setup routine I developed is designed to eliminate 90% of golf swing errors. There is a lot of detail to the routine and I explain why each detail must be followed. If there was a part of the routine that wasn't needed, I cut it out and what remains, if followed in detail does just what I say it will do...

The setup routine works if you follow it in detail.

But if you decide to take shortcuts, I can usually trace your golf swing errors back to problems that start at setup. Again, follow the setup routine in detail.

I also get emails from golfers who have been struggling with the same problem for a long time... But they never asked me about it! The simple fact is that I can help, but only if I know all of the facts of the situation. If you email me, tell me everything you believe might be related to the problem, including the type of practice you do. You'll be surprised at how the little details will tell me what is happening.

This book is about your golf GAME, not just your golf swing. I will show you how to gain control of both your movement and your mind.

Although my methods show fast results, you must consistently practice what you learn to make sure you remember all of the details that make it work and habitually include them in your routines.

My instruction looks very simple at first. It is, but there are details that must be followed to make it work. Pay attention to the details of this instruction. The details are what make the instruction work so well.

Don't try to fix your whole game at one time. First and foremost, <u>balance comes first</u>. Until monitoring balance during your setup routine and swing is an automatic function, anything you try to fix in your mental game will probably not work.

Many golfers decide to stick to technique instruction while trying to add the idea of balance. That's a problem because technique does not take balance into affect and usually throws balance off. If you insist on working on technique: **Allow your balance to adjust your technique and you will have the best of both worlds.**

When you do your pre-round warm up, balance comes first, then timing, and only afterward, the mental side of focus and control.

Be patient. The golf swing can seem complicated due to the many minor details that can make it or break it. If something isn't working at first, let it go and go back to what was working until you can review the instruction and see what details you missed.

The only time to make adjustments is when your previous adjustments have become a consistent habit.

You are going to ask yourself why in the world there are no pictures or illustrations in this book. It's NOT because I'm lazy. There is a method to this madness.

As I mentioned before, after 4 years of teaching golfers world-wide using just the original Golf Swing Control Manual plus email coaching, a company came along and made an offer to create a DVD set to go along with the manual.

When new customers started receiving their course packages with the DVDs, more golfers than ever complained that they weren't seeing results. After some research, I found that even with very obvious instructions letting golfers know why they needed to read the manual before viewing the DVDs, only a small percentage of them did.

I also realized that reading the book prompted golfers to visualize what they read, while watching DVDs, which were very professionally done, did the opposite. I have since reverted to teaching average golfers using only the Golf Swing Control Manual and once again, the results are better than they were with DVDs.

So, the reason there are no pictures or illustrations is twofold. First, I want you to start using your imagination to visualize what you read. Second, every bit of this information is already in video form online in one of my websites. If you are an average golfer, you would go to:

www.golfswingcontrol.com.

An advanced golfer would go to:

www.biovisualfocus.com

You are probably also wondering where the table of contents is… Sorry, but it is left out, as are page numbers, so you don't skip around. I want you to read this book in its entirety because every part is related to the rest. These are not tips or stand alone chapters. This book is designed to build your game mentally and physically from the inside out. It is best to BOOKMARK any points you want to remember and review later. It will also help to bookmark points you don't understand so you can ask about them as well.

There is something very interesting about the learning process that I realized after Golf Swing Control was in print for a year.

Once golfers started reading Golf Swing Control and applying the information, the overwhelming positive response told me that this information was definitely needed by many golfers, but after a year or so I started getting a different kind of email response. It was an even bigger WOW response from golfers who went back to review the manual.

Golfers who went back and reviewed the manual told me that they picked up as much new information

during subsequent readings as they did on the first reading.

What happened?

During the first reading of Golf Swing Control, golfers picked up the information they were ready to receive given the state of their golf game at the time. Once they progressed and the new information became habit, they were ready for more advanced information, which was there, except it just didn't make sense during the first reading.

To get the most from this instruction, review this material when you feel comfortable with your game improvements. You may be very surprised at the new information you'll see.

One more thing; **remember that I am a well trained former Military Interrogator.** (Which is the hard way to get a psychology degree.) I understand how the mind operates and how you will learn the quickest. I may ask you to do something that doesn't make sense. I need you to trust that I have your best interest at heart. Try everything with an open mind and I think you will have a whole new perspective on the game of golf.

Just reading the material will not help you. You must get out and try everything to experience it and develop questions. Then read the areas where you have questions to finally understand the material. Once you have read, experienced, and then read the material again, you can always email me if you still don't get it.

You will also see certain information repeated throughout the book. Instead of wondering why I keep repeating myself, please pay closer attention to those points. Certain points have been repeated because those are the most common places golfers make mistakes and I want to make sure you don't make the same mistakes.

Lastly, I wrote this book to help you have fun. Golf is a frustrating game if you have to work at it. Even the pros on tour have to let go of the work part and have fun to play well. If it is your goal to play on the PGA Tour, and that goal is realistic, call me. I'll be glad to help.

What is Golf's Last Barrier?

Three holes to play and you're one off the lead. A couple of good holes and you could be the club champion. Your game is working its best ever. The tee shot is an easy one. You set up, take your normal swing and, "What the $#@%^?" A snarf shot out of bounds...

Watch the PGA Tour. Tour golfers are truly talented. They work hard on their games and they have the very best resources available to them. Yet despite all of the technology, all of the advances in golf swing theory and all of the mental game work, they are still somewhat inconsistent. Just like all of the amateur golfers who watch them on TV, they have good days and bad days. On bad days they might be playing well when the game suddenly falls apart. Golfers who have a chance to take the lead fall apart in their moment of opportunity. Golfers who sleep on an overnight lead often struggle the next day.

You don't have to play on tour or even be a professional golfer to experience this phenomenon. When you are playing so well that you feel like you finally have this game in hand and suddenly everything goes bad... Well I think we've all been there at one time. It is probably the worst feeling you can have on a golf course.

Most golfers wonder for days, weeks or months what is wrong with their golf swing. They go to the range and try to work it out, knowing in the back of their mind it can still happen anytime... Without a clue as to why it happens.

And when the breakdown happens, when does your golf game suddenly recover?

I know that for me, my game used to recover just after my score was so bad that I didn't care about the round any more... That's just the golf gods pouring salt in your wounds.

But if you are in a tournament or playing a match, what can you do? You don't want to give up! You have to do *something*!

The mental coaching gurus will tell you that your problem is all in your head. You were probably thinking about swing technique and your conscious mind got in the way. <u>And they are correct</u>...

But what happens when you're <u>not</u> thinking about swing technique and the swing <u>still isn't</u> working? You have two choices. You can either <u>not</u> think about swing technique and continue to hit crappy shots, or you can try to do *SOMETHING* to hit the ball better; But what?

Until now, the only choice was to try to get your golf swing working, which means thinking about swing technique.

We've all experienced the downward spiral that happens when we start thinking about the golf swing, but what other choice is there?

If you can't think about your golf swing, what do you do when nothing is working?

That IS the question isn't it?

That is golf's last barrier.

I have presented this to many mental coaches without ever getting a good answer.

The REAL problem is that the swing you have practiced for thousands of hours (if you are a pro) isn't working <u>and your mind wants to know why</u>. If you've played for any period of time, you have experienced this too many times and your mind just wants to know why in hell you can't find a golf swing that will just work!

This is why golfers get frustrated to the point of throwing, bending, and breaking golf clubs. Above all else, your brain does one thing for you 24/7 <u>that you can't shut off</u>. It tries to solve all of your problems. The more a problem shows up, the harder the brain works to solve it.

How can you <u>not</u> think at a time like that?

When tour golfers are having a bad day they will sometimes go to the driving range after the round to figure out the problem.

But think about this for a second... Is the problem really their golf swing?

It might be for the average golfer but the professional golfer on the range has already played some great rounds of golf and he hits superb shots <u>all of the time</u>. There is no doubt his golf swing works, so what is he working on?

I was watching a tournament on TV. One of the co-leaders has two holes to go and needs only one birdie to win outright. Otherwise he's looking at a playoff. Watching his stance, I can tell the drive was going to the right, and it did. This golfer had been rock solid for the whole tournament, yet when in his mind he only needed to birdie one of the last two holes, the wheels got a little loose. Hmmm...

Another golfer in the same tournament two strokes off of the lead finds himself needing two birdies with four holes to play. It's doable. But he gets up to the tee and his stance was screaming high pop left, which is what he did. This golfer was a veteran on tour who had played very steady until that point. On the next tee, he does it again, but this time he doesn't save the hole. Now, with no possibility of winning he stands on the 17th tee, makes a perfect setup and splits the fairway.

What happened to mess up his swing on the previous two holes?

He wasn't alone. A few other golfers with a chance to tie the lead did similar things.

So, what happened?

Let's just say there was a short-circuit in their brain that caused the wheels to fall off momentarily.

The Last Barrier in golf to conquer is when your mind short-circuits and causes those unexplainable missed shots that send you into the depths of golf hell.

What happens in your mind is similar to when your computer locks up and just stops working. You have to reset it to get it going again. When the computer doesn't reset, you're staring at the "blue screen of death" as it's called by computer geeks. Now and then you can reset your mind on the golf course, but when you're looking at a blue screen of death in your mind, you're in for a long day of grinding out every shot.

It's time to stop blaming your golf swing.

The golf swing has been analyzed to death. Every year there is a new golf swing "system" that is supposed to change golf as we know it, but handicaps don't change and the best golfers in the world still only win a few times per year.

Think back to the times before the golf instruction revolution. Arnold Palmer, Jack Nicklaus, Gary Player all had unique golf swings. They practiced what worked for them and they didn't constantly look for a more efficient swing method. They focused on hitting shots on the golf course and scoring. Since they weren't focused on their golf swing, they didn't get locked up mentally coming down the last nine holes of the tournament. In fact, during the last nine holes of the

tournament, they actually sharpened their focus and played
<u>better</u>!

So, what has changed from the "good ole days of golf"
until now? What is happening in the minds of present day
golfers that causes a lockup for even the very best pros on
tour?

Every movement a person makes from simple to more
complicated tasks requires a set of instructions from the
mind passed to the muscles of the body to create that
movement. Even if you are just walking, something you do
without conscious thought, instructions pass from the
subconscious mind to the body. Whether it's walking or the
golf swing, the body does exactly what it is told to do. Those
instructions come from the brain's memory through the
subconscious mind.

When you experience this mental glitch there is a loss of
communication between the mind and body. Think about
when you trip while walking... Isn't usually just after you have
been distracted by something? A small distraction can do the
same thing to your golf swing. During a glitch, the golf swing
happens but the accuracy is gone because the instructions to
the body for your golf swing are broken up due to poor
communications from the mind to the body.

Sometimes a golfer will find himself in the zone and have
an incredible round. Then, the next day his mind gets stuck
somewhere and par golf becomes a struggle. Outside of the

occasion when a golfer finds himself in the zone, those few down to the wire mistakes are made when something in the golfer's mind short-circuits. Many times it costs the lead or a win.

This is the area of golf that very few have broken through: **Finding and solving this glitch is golf's last barrier.**

For today's mental coaches, the search for the zone is the best way to prevent those few blow-up moments caused by mental glitches because those glitches don't happen in the Zone.

In fact, trying to get golfers into the Zone is the only way mental coaches have come up with so far to keep a golfer from choking coming down to the wire. Mental coaches often tout that they can train a golfer to get into the Zone, yet it is still only sporadic. It seems to me that if they could consistently place a golfer in the Zone, one golfer would have taken the golf world by storm by now, but that isn't happening. Tiger was as close as we have seen lately and at his best he still struggles with his mental game.

I believe the difficulties golfers experience are inherent with the way golfers are trained. In modern golf instruction, the golf swing and the mental game are being trained as separate parts of the game...

But what controls the body?

The mind controls the body. For the best results, the mind and body have to work together.

Splitting up the mind and body is like driving your car blindfolded! The solution is to <u>train</u> the mind and the body together.

Training the golf swing and the mental game together requires breaking through the mental process of movement and combining it with the mental process of thought so that the two parts work together. This is a unified mental /physical approach to the game of golf.

It's taken the better part of 25 years to figure out, but if you understand this glitch, you can take measures to prevent it, and if it does show up, you know what to do to fix it so the glitch doesn't ruin your day.

Fixing this mental glitch also helps your physical golf game. The average golfer will find an effective golf swing that fits his or her body. The advanced golfer will see better accuracy and consistent distance. All of the information you need will be found in this book.

When it comes down to it, fixing this glitch will address your complete golf game from the inside-out. It may sound like a monumental task, but it's actually quite simple as long as you have the correct perspective of the game of golf. If you follow the 4-step program in this book, you will have the answers you are looking for, and your golf game will be stress free and enjoyable. It's all in this book, but beware; this is not your standard golf instruction.

These are real solutions you can use for the rest of your golfing days.

The Traps that Create the Glitch

Golf is assuredly a mystifying game. It would seem that if a person has hit a golf ball correctly a thousand times, he should be able to duplicate the performance at will. But such is certainly not the case. – Bobby Jones

Even the great Bobby Jones fell victim to the glitch...

Before you can solve a problem, you have to identify it and understand it. In this case the problem is a mental glitch that happens on the golf course wreaking havoc with the games of golfers the world over.

The glitch consists of two parts:

1. The moment when your golf swing fails to deliver consistently.
2. The moment when your conscious mind decides it <u>has</u> to know <u>why</u> it is happening.

It is also known that practiced properly, your golf swing gets stored in the motor cortex (your brain's hard drive) and like a program in a computer, gets loaded into the subconscious (RAM) where the instructions are sent through the neural network to signal your muscles to make the golf swing.

If you've ever made perfect golf shots, you know the instructions are all there, so what happens that the muscles don't always do what they are supposed to do?

The most common reason for this glitch and the one I always address first is that <u>your brain scrapped the golf swing program</u> because you were out of balance during the golf swing. This "scrapping the program" is a subconscious automatic action that most golfers are completely unaware is wrecking their golf game.

Balance is an automatic function that affects even the best golfers in the world. If during movement, you are not in a state of dynamic balance, and the brain can't get you back there with minor adjustments, the brain abandons the current movement program as needed and takes more drastic measures to get your body back into a state of balance as you move, which unfortunately alters the intended movement, in this case, screwing up your golf swing. This auto-balance program is wired into your DNA, so there's no training that will allow you to work around it.

The second reason the muscles wouldn't get the golf swing program from the brain is that something in your mind stopped the transmission. It's a lot like a smart phone that slows down because another program is running in the background. In the case of the golfer, he has other thoughts slowing down or stopping the communication between the golf swing program and the muscles. Any extra conscious thoughts will do that. They start to snowball when doubt gets involved and can completely freeze up your brain.

A mental coach will blame <u>all</u> of your issues on the second problem, thinking about extra stuff, but often the extra stuff, usually technical thoughts about your swing, will start <u>because of a balance issue throwing off your golf swing</u>.

Any variation in your golf shots can cause you to start wondering what is wrong. Those conscious thoughts act like the background program slowing down your smart phone, but in this case they would be interrupting your calls.

The third reason for the glitch is that you are distracted by non-technical conscious thoughts. You should leave these thoughts in the parking lot before the round, but it can be difficult. There are ways to deal with these thoughts when they show up, but this is the one purely mental issue of the three glitch causes.

How do you cure the glitch?

1. The process of eliminating this glitch starts with balance. Start the swing in balance and swing in dynamic balance. This is of major importance because your subconscious will automatically ditch the swing if you are not moving in dynamic balance. There is no choice here; it's just how your brain is wired.

2. Simplify the golf swing and get the timing right.

3. Build routines using active awareness to coordinate the two minds for the shot process.

4. Use active awareness to eliminate extraneous thoughts interrupting the process.

I'm going to take you through this 4-step process to eliminate your glitch and break through your golf barrier.

Golf Swing Technique – The Ultimate Distraction

You swing your best when you have the fewest things to think about. – Bobby Jones

Why do I say that technique is the ultimate distraction?

During the process of learning or changing movement, technique thoughts are conscious thoughts. As you will see, conscious thoughts are the enemy to your golf swing.

I worked with 1000's of students over the last 20 years. In almost every case, the difference between breaking through to a better game was whether or not the student would let go of their technical swing thoughts.

I have taken students out to the range and had them think of nothing other than balance and seen almost instant transformations in their swings. Fast golf swings have better timing. Fidgety golfers become more comfortable over the golf ball. Arm swingers start using their body during the golf swing.

I have taken students to the golf course and walked with them, reminding them to only feel for balance during their round and have seen these students fire amazing rounds the day after shooting some of their worst scores. And remember, balance is just the start!

I have seen those same students turn around and immediately go back to working on technique and find them struggling again with the game I thought we had eradicated.

It doesn't make sense.

Think about this: <u>During a golf shot</u>, how do you positively know where your golf club is pointing at the top of the backswing? Do you really know at the top of the backswing (without looking) if your club is on plane? Can you think about your swing plane and wrist position at the same time? If so, do you know if your backswing is finishing completely?

The fact is, the way technical instruction is taught; there is no way to know if your swing is on plane or your wrist position is correct. The instructor places you in "the correct" position and it's up to you to figure out how to get back there again every time you swing the club.

To make things worse, if you use video to review your golf swing, you are looking at what is happening on the outside of your body. That is the *result* of the movement process. Trying to fix the result never fixes the process that creates the result. It just doesn't make sense.

There *is* a way to make sure all aspects of your swing are correct without actually thinking about them, but that method is rarely taught during technical instruction.

I have had students who came back to me after technique had crept back into their brains and ruined their games to once again play amazing golf based mainly on balance. Some stay that way, but for some reason completely unknown to me, too many go back. It's as if technique was an addiction to golfers!

Mental Coaches on the PGA Tour teach their golfers that technical thoughts will kill their game. They are correct. Again, technical thoughts are conscious thoughts, and conscious thoughts are bad for your golf game if not handled properly.

Tour players go to a swing coach who works on their technique and then go to a mental coach who is telling them not to think about technique. It doesn't make sense but it is a testament to their talent as they somehow keep playing at the top of their games.

How do they do it? In most cases I have found that the processes I will make you aware of in this book are happening for these golfers naturally in the background of their mind <u>but without their awareness</u>. Of course, this only becomes an issue when the processes stop or get interrupted and the golfer has no clue what has happened.

By making you aware of the processes that happen behind the scenes during your golf swing, I am giving you the tools you will need to fix things as soon as your golf swing even hints at a glitch.

Nowadays, my first test to see if a golfer is truly committed to making the PGA Tour is the "technique test". I show them how balance and timing will instantly place their golf swing right where they need it. I then take them to the golf course and continue proving it by showing them how something so simple can allow them to play amazing golf. Once I'm sure they understand, I give them a week or two to practice. Once the practice time is through, I see what they are working on. If it's technique, I explain the test and ask if they think they can kick the habit.

Unfortunately, most golfers refuse to let go of their technique based golf swing thoughts, often telling me how they are "so close". They don't realize that they will continue to spend most of their golfing days, convinced that they are always "so close". This simple mindset shift is the real difference between making and not making it on the PGA Tour.

This book is about how to let go of technique and engage your subconscious to make controlled, powerful, yet free-flowing golf swings and golf shots that will amaze you. It is the answer to the question all golfers ask, **"How do you NOT think about technique and still play well?"**

It's still possible to go through this book, use all of this information and still think about technique. <u>Unfortunately, you won't break through that way</u>.

If you want to break through to your best game, you have to let go of technique.

The Downfall of Gadgets

It's a funny thing, the more I practice the luckier I get.
– Arnold Palmer

Modern golf instruction has graduated to using gadgets, video analysis and computers to decide how you should make your golf swing. I want you to think about these contraptions and then mentally take yourself out to the golf course. What good are they when you are actually playing golf?

If an instructor spends weeks working on getting your plane just right, how do you positively know while you are hitting a shot on the golf course if you have the correct plane? If you aren't sure, there is no way to know because you don't have the video camera out there nor do you have the instructor constantly adjusting you. You just have you. If the shots aren't working, you will start wondering if your swing plane is correct. <u>Those doubts in your mind will wreck your game</u>.

Some good instructors I know have created a computer guided training system where you can track your swing live as you make it. The idea is that you record the track you want to swing along using sensors on your body and golf club and once it is recorded, you can slowly make your golf swing and follow the exact swing path every time. This program is designed to build the myelination of the neurons that have to fire for your golf swing. It's a very ingenious invention and they are doing very well with it. Again, the only downfall is that once trained, you have no choice but to trust it out on the golf course. If the swing isn't producing results, what do you do?

Most gadgets are designed to restrict your movement so that the muscles have no choice but to follow the same path. This method tries to follow the same theory of myelination of neurons, but there is a problem. If you strap on some kind of gadget or swing in an apparatus that restricts your movement, what are your muscles doing while you are using the gadget? Your muscles are working <u>against</u> the gadget. in essence, your muscles are relying on the gadget to make things right. But if you are training the muscles to work against a gadget, what will they do when the gadget comes off? When you think you are training your muscles to do one thing, the restriction actually tells the muscles to do the opposite. This is why gadgets often have an opposite effect.

Why am I telling you all of this?

Because you have a super computer already built into your brain and body. You also have a video camera already working for you in your brain. You can take them both to the golf course with you and know exactly what is happening at all times with your golf swing. You can have them anywhere you need them to make sure you play the golf game you want to play without the anxiety and worry about the possibility of a breakdown on the golf course that you can't work through.

This book will teach you how to use your own built-in super computer to create your best, most efficient, natural golf swing and keep it working anywhere.

The Lynch Pin

Keep your sense of humor. There's enough stress in the rest of your life not to let bad shots ruin a game you're supposed to enjoy – Amy Alcott

So, what is the big secret? What is the lynch pin that connects the mental and physical side of golf?

What happens when you are walking and suddenly catch your foot on something?

Doesn't your body automatically do whatever it can to stop you from falling?

The key word is AUTOMATICALLY...

The lynch pin is a sneaky little program in your mind that demands that your body stay in balance at all times. Before you shake your head in disbelief, let me explain in simple terms. I will get into more detail in the next chapter.

Your brain has a built in auto-balance mechanism that works 24/7. If you are out of balance, your mind immediately takes action to right the ship. In most sports, it isn't a big deal because your mind keeps you in balance with tiny adjustments every time you make a step.

In golf, you don't move your feet when you hit the golf ball. What that means is that your mind will do something else if you are not in balance during your golf swing. In the case of the golf swing, the mind adjusts muscle dynamics to keep you in balance, but in the process throws the golf swing off. That's the physical side…

On the mental side you have to deal with the subconscious mind. The subconscious mind is the mind that controls movement. It is known by sports mental coaches that it is the conscious mind that messes up athletes by getting involved and interrupting focus during movement.

In other words, to play your best golf, your mind should be in a subconscious state when you swing the golf club. It's actually not that difficult once you know the requirements, which I will go into detail on in a later chapter.

Remember the auto-balance program? Well, when the auto balance program has to kick in during the golf swing because you are not in dynamic balance, **the program also closes the door to the subconscious.**

If you *are* moving in balance, the subconscious is ready willing and able to assist you in making a perfect golf swing.

It's not simple balance, but <u>the dynamic auto-balance program</u> hard wired into your brain that is the lynch pin you must master if you ever want to play top level golf.

I will go on to prove this to you and show you how to be one with your auto-balance programming so you can find the zone and hit perfect golf shots all day long. OK... Almost perfect!

The Importance of Static and Dynamic Balance

When you start driving your ball down the middle, you meet a different class of people. – Phil Harris, comedian

Humans are hard-wired to stay in balance. It is a built-in automatic self preservation mechanism. If you are walking and suddenly trip, without thought the brain takes control of the body and you instantly react. That reaction is your subconscious trying to rebalance your body. There is no choice in the matter.

In just about every sport, your feet constantly change positions; you step, walk or run and when you move, the brain uses those opportunities to quickly adjust and balance your body. In most sports dynamic balance works <u>for you</u> without thought because your movement facilitates the act of balancing.

In golf, this same automatic balance system usually works AGAINST you. Because your feet don't move, your brain has to make a <u>whole different set of adjustments</u> to stay in balance. Because your feet don't move, the automatic balance system will adjust how the muscles work. Those adjustments make balance more important in golf than in other sports because changing muscle dynamics changes the golf swing.

Golf is a unique sport because you start from a static balance position and once you start your golf swing you fall under the laws of dynamic balance. The properties of static balance and dynamic balance are different. A golfer in dynamic balance also fulfills the laws of static balance, but not the other way around.

Static balance is balance over a point such as a big rock balanced and sitting on a smaller rock. As long as the big rock isn't affected by an outside force, it doesn't move. As soon as the big rock is moved, gravity takes over and the big rock falls. While you are in a stationary position, as long as you don't fall down, you are statically balanced

Dynamic balance is balance during motion, or how humans and animals balance themselves while moving. The difference between golf and most other sports when it comes to dynamic balance (once again) is that your feet don't change positions during the golf swing. In other sports the movement, lifting and replacing the feet gives the brain plenty of places to make the automatic balance adjustments that can't be made during a golf swing.

To demonstrate how static balance and dynamic balance work for a golfer, Imagine trying to keep your feet in one place and have someone push you enough to be off balance. (Imagine two Sumo wrestlers battling it out)

While your mind tries to fight the outside force to stay in balance, you will feel your body adjust the tension in certain muscles, depending on how you were pushed. If you are pushed too far you will have to move one or both feet to keep from falling down.

One reason humans have muscles is to counteract gravity, so if you are in balance and then you are acted on by an outside force, your muscles will make adjustments to keep you from falling. Try standing up with your knees straight and bending forward from the waist. Notice how the muscles in the back of your legs tighten up to counteract the extra weight in the front of your body. In this case you are statically balanced, but since the opposing muscles are working out of balance with each other, you are not dynamically balanced.

Now try standing with your knees bent and bend forward. Your backside should move back to counter your forward bend. In this case your body is using weight to counter weight and opposing muscle groups are working evenly with each other. In this case you are both statically and dynamically balanced. This is the preferred balance method the body will use provided you allow it.

The difference between the two exercises was the straight knees vs. the bent knees. When you straighten your knees, you tighten the muscles in the front of your legs. The opposing muscles in the back of your legs are free to counter the muscles in the front of your legs up to a point. Because the locked knees force certain muscles of your legs to work harder than their opposing muscles, you are dynamically unbalanced. In the bent knee exercise, you are using the front and back muscles together, so when you bend, they act evenly to counter the weight. The second exercise demonstrates dynamic balance at work.

Dynamic balance is the balancing of opposing muscle groups in the body during movement as a reaction to gravity.

If you start your golf swing from a position that is <u>not</u> BOTH statically and dynamically balanced, your brain will immediately start making unplanned adjustments to your muscles in an attempt to regain a state of dynamic balance in response to the brain's auto-balance mechanism.

When the brain attempts to rebalance your body during your golf swing, the muscles you intend to use to hit the golf ball are now reassigned to balance, <u>which changes the course of your golf swing</u>.

This subtle act of trying to achieve dynamic balance happens without your awareness <u>and is the most common reason for 90% of all technical golf swing problems</u>. There is no stopping dynamic balance, so as a golfer you must work with it.

Think about what happens when your balance is a little off and your shots aren't going where you intend them to go.

In your mind, you start wondering if something is wrong with your golf swing.

Being out of balance during the golf swing is the biggest reason golfers start thinking technical swing thoughts during a round of golf.

IMPORTANT: These balance issues CANNOT be fixed with technical golf swing instruction.

Golf swing balance irregularities are the core reason technical golf swing instruction doesn't last. You can use all of the different golf swing styles you want; if your body isn't in balance during your golf swing, your brain will try to adjust the muscles of your body to get back into balance, which will alter <u>any</u> golf swing.

The need to get both static and dynamic balance right at the same time is why the setup routine I created took so long to develop and why doing it properly eliminates so many swing errors. I had to find a foolproof stance routine that is both statically and dynamically balanced.

Once you are in balance, you will find one more huge benefit. I discovered it when I created Golf Swing Control, but didn't realize how important it was for golfers until I developed Bio-Visual Focus for advanced golfers.

Balance opens the door to access your subconscious mind, which is the door to the Zone.

When I started getting emails from Golf Swing Control members telling me that they were seeing their own golf swing moving in their mind <u>during their golf swing</u>, I knew there was more to balance than I had figured. Many described their visuals as if they were watching their own body from the inside out. It sounded a little weird, but I had experienced the same thing.

Looking further into this phenomenon, I realized that any <u>access to the subconscious gets blocked if the subconscious mind is busy trying to place you back into dynamic balance</u>. This is why the Zone is so difficult to get into. On the other hand, if you are moving in dynamic balance, the mind prefers visualization over conscious thought and the subconscious (the Zone) is available.

This phenomenon explains why even PGA tour golfers sometimes struggle during play. When they are playing slightly out of balance, the shots don't go as planned and visualization is difficult. This often leads to technical golf swing thoughts in an effort to right the ship. The result is a tough day grinding it out on the golf course.

I always address balance first with every student I teach. I find that fixing balance also repairs many of the other mistakes that golfers make, which makes adjusting the rest of the golf swing easy. Understanding balance helps you understand the full importance of getting each detail of the setup routine in this book right and makes your improvement happen very quickly.

The Paradox of Playing by Feel

A quick note about "feel" players: When you are moving in dynamic balance, the muscles are working evenly with their opposing muscle groups, so there is NO feel that stands out in your body. So if your golf swing depends on feeling certain muscles work, you are swinging out of balance. It's another reason the Zone is so hard to pinpoint.

The Perfect Golf Swing Stance and Grip Routine

The reason the pro tells you to keep your head down is so you can't see him laughing. - Phyllis Diller

Many Tour Professional players say that when they are having a bad day, they never felt relaxed in their setup routine. If the grip, knee-bend, spine angle, or any other part of the setup is off by just a little bit, the setup will feel "off" and directly affect the golf swing.

What do you think about when you set up to the ball?

- Do you wonder if your knees are bent too much, or not enough?
- Do you look to see if your hands are too close or too far away from the body?
- Does your grip feel a little off?

These are common conscious thoughts that will hurt your golf swing before you ever move the golf club.

When you are out on the golf course, you can't see your setup, so if you want to know it is right <u>you have to learn to feel it and absolutely know if it is correct</u>. If your setup is not right, you need to know how to fix it so you don't suffer the consequences of dynamic balance. This routine is designed to take all of the conscious thought out of setting up perfectly for every golf shot. As a result, this golf grip and stance routine will <u>automatically place you in a properly balanced stance for any golf club or any golf shot</u>.

More importantly: This routine automatically adjusts to your body's build, so it doesn't matter how tall or short, big or small you are.

WARNING: You must pay attention to all of the details or this routine won't help you. There are a lot of details, but believe me, I already removed anything that wasn't needed.

The routine I teach now took 12 years to develop and test so that it will work whether you are 4'9" or 7'2" and will automatically adjust your setup for whatever club you are holding.

Before I go into the grip routine, I want to illustrate how important the grip is. When I was working in Myrtle Beach, I was practicing one windy fall day and the only other golfer on the range was a professional from the golf course across the street. I was hitting low wind cheaters into a stiff breeze and he was trying to do the same.

He was getting ready for the Greater Greensboro Open and with the change of weather he knew he would have to hit lower shots. His shots were ballooning and in frustration he asked me to see if I could tell why. After about 15 minutes watching his swing I told him I couldn't see anything that would cause the issue, and then I saw his glove hand...

His glove had the classic palm hole that comes from gripping the club with the end of the club inside the grip rather than past the grip. I pointed his grip out and he said that if he gripped the club with the end past his hand, he wouldn't hit the ball clean.

His grip was compromised because his setup routine placed him too far away from the ball to reach comfortably, so he adjusted his grip. One mistake led to another causing loss of ball control on his shots.

After a short discussion, I showed him the setup routine to get his body position where is should be and adjusted his grip. In a few minutes he was hitting low wind cheaters that would take him around even the windiest golf course.

The grip

This grip description is for right handed golfers. Lefties will have to reverse left and right in the descriptions.

To get your grip:

> Hold your golf club in the fingers of your target side hand on the target side of your body so that your elbow is touching your body. Your arm from the elbow to the hand is parallel to the ground and the club is also parallel to the ground. The toe of the club should be pointing straight up. For an iron the leading edge of the club should be pointing straight up. For a wood the top face edge will be pointing straight up.

Reach across your body with your opposite hand, keeping the club lined up with the target side of your body. The elbow of the reaching arm should be against the body. Slip the middle two fingers under the grip below the target side hand but up against the index finger of the target side hand.

Grip the club in the fingers of the reaching hand while allowing the fingers of the target side hand to grip the club as well.

There is a groove in the base of the right hand that fits perfectly over the left thumb. Make sure those parts are joined.

A Note: Gripping in the fingers gives you free and total control of the golf club. It eliminates tension in the wrists and arms that would reduce your ability to transfer energy to the golf ball. It also allows the wrists to naturally turn and hinge through the hitting area without having to be forced to do so, eliminating blocked shots often caused by tight wrists.

The pinky finger of the reaching hand can either overlap the target side index finger, it can interlock with the index finger or you can try my personal grip…

I was constantly fighting my grip for years. Some days I couldn't seem to stop myself from gripping the club too strong and other days I was too weak. There was no "standard" that set my grip the same way every time until I tried my current grip. There is only one small change to a standard Vardon grip, but it makes all of the difference once you get used to feeling it. I put the very tip of the pinky finger of my right hand against the grip inside the "V" formed between the first two fingers of the target side hand. I find that doing this keeps me from sliding the right hand under or over the target side hand so my grip is always the same. It prevents grip related shot errors. This small adjustment also makes it easier to keep the grip from slipping into the palms.

The thumb of the reaching or "away" hand goes across the top of the grip and touches the tip of the index finger of the same hand. The "V" between the thumb and index finger of the away hand should be pinched closed. If you can't pinch the V closed, it means you have the club gripped in your palm rather than your fingers.

I'd like to mention some notable details about the golf grip.

- The butt of the grip should extend just past the heel of the left hand (right handed golfers). Usually there is a line about 1/8 inch before the end of the grip that should be visible when gripping the club. This helps to maintain control of the club, prevents the glove wearing out in the palm (a telltale sign),

and helps to keep your shots from ballooning
when you're trying to keep them low.

- The club should be gripped lightly in the fingers.
  The fingers of your hand are much stronger and
  react much quicker to the increasing forces of the
  downswing than the palm. Gripping the club in the
  palm requires more work to hold the club, which
  means more tension. That tension will stop the
  wrists from hinging properly near impact. The
  further into the palm of the hand the club is
  gripped, the more likely you are to hit some shots
  with the club face wide open for no explainable
  reason.

- The right thumb should NOT be on top of the club.
  Placing the thumb on top of the club creates
  tension that goes all the way to the shoulder.
  Tension in the grip will rob power from the golf
  swing.

- The connection between the groove in the base of
  the right palm and the left thumb needs to be solid
  for better club control and power.

Try this experiment: grip a club in your palm with the
right thumb on top of the grip and push down with the
thumb. You should be able to feel the tension all the way up
the right arm and through part of your back. That tension is a
swing killer.

The stance routine that I teach works very well in just about every case. I have experimented with it by showing golfers at a driving range nothing more than the basics of the routine. When they properly performed this drill, their shots stayed on line with the intended target.

First, step up to the ball with the away (from the target) foot, bend forward from the hips (don't hunch over) and ground the club head behind the ball. Keep 90% of your weight on the ball of your away foot (specifically behind the big toe) and tilt your upper body forward until your arms are hanging straight down from your shoulders and you have about a hand's width clearance from your legs. Only the toe of your target side foot is touching the ground while setting the club. This part of the routine sets your distance to the golf ball and the forward tilt of your body from the waist.

Take note of the height of your hands relative to your thighs. Your hands should be about half way between your knees and hips or a little lower. This is what I call the power band. If you stand too tall and your hands are too high on your legs, you only engage the tiny muscles around your hips. If you are too low, your knees will want to move around and you will find yourself raising up during the backswing.

It is important to keep your chin up and your back straight rather than hunched over at this point.

Keeping the weight on the ball of the away foot while placing the club forces your upper body to find the correct forward bend.

Once you get the angle of waist bend/forward upper body tilt, it is very important to keep that angle and posture while you place the rest of your body.

The next step is the most important: While keeping the club grounded behind the ball, look down range at your target, and keeping the upper body angle intact, place your target side foot and then move your away foot into place so that your weight is distributed evenly in the arches of your feet. Continue looking downrange. Move back and forth, foot to foot, in small steps (actually taking the whole foot off of the ground) until your body feels comfortable with your weight centered in the arches of your feet. This movement should be made without swinging the hips, but rather keeping the hips centered and rocking foot to foot as you pick up and place your feet. Each foot should leave the ground each time you step.

The key here is to consciously feel the weight distribution under the arches of your feet as you rock from foot to foot while continuing to look downrange. The club should still be grounded behind the ball at this point. This part of the routine makes small adjustments for your distance to the ball and places your body in both static and dynamic balance.

Do not reach for the ball with your arms, even with a driver. This places the body out of balance, which will lock up the lower body and make a mess of your golf swing. The arms should hang naturally from the shoulders.

The weight felt under the feet should always be in the arches of the feet at setup and under the inside halves of the bottoms of the feet during the swing.

If during the swing, your weight gets to the outside of either foot before the ball is struck, your subconscious will perceive that as an out of balance situation and take automatic action that will hurt the golf swing.

DO NOT look back at the ball until your feet are positioned and you feel comfortable!!! AGAIN, all placement of the feet is performed while you are looking down range at your target with the club grounded behind the ball.

I always get questions from golfers asking me how to know where to place their feet if they aren't looking down to see where they are relative to the ball and their target line.

You should be visualizing in your mind where the ball is relative to your feet to "see" in your mind where to place your feet. This jump starts the visualization process and keeps you relaxed for your golf swing.

If you don't get it correct right away, back off and do this step again until you feel comfortable with the process. Every time you do this part of the setup, you will notice that your visualization of the ball as you place your feet improves.

Since your away hand is lower on the grip, your away shoulder should be lower than your target side shoulder. A big mistake golfers make here is to just drop the shoulder. Instead, this is accomplished by tilting the spine from the hips slightly away from the target. It is important to keep the spine straight but tilted. Golfers who just drop the shoulder are placing their spine in a curved condition that makes the backswing more difficult to manage.

For a standard swing style, as you tilt away from the target, you should also feel the weight felt under the feet shift from 50% on each foot to about 65% felt under the arch of the away foot.

For a Stack and Tilt style of golf swing, keep the weight centered while tilting.

How much should you tilt?

A good test of the proper tilt is to get your stance, release your away hand from the grip, and allow your away arm to hang straight down naturally from the shoulder, swing the arm away from the golf club and back to it allowing gravity to keep the arm hanging straight up and down. If the hand goes back to the proper place on the grip, the tilt is good. If the hand is too low, you tilted too much and if the hand is too high on the grip when it swings back, you tilted too little.

As well, if your hand is the proper height but does not line up with your hand/grip position when it swings back, your hands are either too close or too far from your body.

Why should you tilt?

- Setting the spine angle to the right (tilting away from the target) sets your away hip in the proper position so you can turn your upper body without sliding or swaying the hips during the backswing.
- This also allows a coiling on the away side leg, where much of the energy is stored during the backswing.
- The alignment of your shoulders and arms with the target is also accommodated by tilting away from the target. Without the tilt you would be open to the target.

Without the tilt, you are guaranteed to have a sway in your golf swing because the away hip will lock before the backswing turn is even half way complete. This will usually force the away leg to lock out as well, which is also a serious power and balance loss. With the arms and shoulders out of line, having no tilt is also one of the biggest reasons for the dreaded over-the-top move that creates lost golf balls to the right.

Again, a very common mistake I see with golfers is to point their arms at the ball when using a wood. This is an out of balance situation that locks up the lower body and can lead to an over-the-top swing. The arms should hang straight down directly under the shoulders because this is where gravity will fight to take them during the downswing. <u>This includes the Driver</u>.

If you feel like your hands are too close to your body, (The grip position should be about the width of your hand across your fingers away from your legs) it means you do not have the proper forward upper body tilt or you are hunched over rather than bent from the hips.

When you start the club in the proper position, you don't have to fight the laws of physics during the swing and you have more energy to direct to the golf ball.

Why look away from the ball when setting the feet?

The reason you look away when you set your feet is to force your auto-balance system to place your body in both static and dynamic balance for the golf swing. If you look at the ball when you set your feet, your conscious mind will over-ride the auto balance system and you will probably NOT be in proper balance. While setting the feet and balancing during this phase, you also automatically get the right amount of knee bend.

IMPORTANT: If you balance yourself and find that the club is no longer behind the ball when you look back down, STEP BACK and start over. When you are set in your stance and the club is no longer centered on the ball, it means that you have been reaching a little bit when you put the club behind the ball which creates an off-balance condition and defeats the whole purpose of the routine. When you step back in to address the ball, use gravity to allow the arms to hang down naturally from the shoulders.

Lastly, ball position is handled by remembering only three important rules:

- The club head goes behind the ball.
- The grip/handle should be ahead of the ball (with exception of the Driver). To be more exact, the bottom of the grip should be just ahead of the ball.
- Your hands should be lined up with your target side inner thigh. In that position, the club face should be lined up to the intended target line. If you get the setup and the club face lined up properly, the ball should fly on line.

For a driver, line the ball up with the arch of your target side foot. With the hands lined up to your target side inner thigh, your hands will be behind the ball. Check the club face alignment in that position to insure the ball flies on your target line.

Practice this setup routine <u>away from the range or golf course</u> until it feels natural.

Practice before you go to bed and your mind will continue practicing during your sleep. It's an easy way to get extra practice in without having to fit it into your day.

Remember, the setup is where 90% of swing mistakes start.

Get this setup right and many of your swing frustrations will disappear.

The Only Swing Drill You Need

Out here, it's just you and the ball. – Mike Weir

Without a coach, an instructor beside you, or a video to watch, how do you know what is happening with your golf swing out on the golf course?

All you have is a few visual cues and your ability to feel your body. Unfortunately, depending on how tired you may be, <u>even body feel changes during a round of golf as your muscles get tired</u>.

There *are* feel points your body experiences you can monitor <u>that don't change</u> because they aren't affected by your mental or physical state. They are your body's response to gravity. This drill is designed to use those feel points along with certain presets you CAN control to help you develop a golf swing that repeats without fail under pressure.

This drill saved my golf game by simplifying the greater part of the golf swing and getting my mind away from mechanics, and even though it helped my game, at the time <u>I had no idea of HOW it worked or why it worked</u>. That left me with no choice but to practice the drill and hope it filtered into my swing, which unfortunately it didn't always do. That's the downfall with drills that work if you don't know what makes them work. I have since figured it out and now it works every time.

This is a swing drill that many players on the PGA tour rely on. Further down I will give you a link to a video where Nick Faldo demonstrates it. Ryan Moore played in tournaments on the PGA using this method on the golf course for a whole season.

It's important to understand why this drill works, so make sure you finish this chapter before using the drill.

Before I go into more detail, I want to clarify the difference between technique and feel. This is important because the level of detail I go into with the swing drill may make you think that I am giving you technique. So here's the difference…

Technique is a movement that cannot be repeated or felt exactly the same way every time because there is no CONSISTENT feedback that tells you the movement is correct without looking at it.

The information I am giving you is tied to consistent feedback methods that will inform you about the correctness of the movement.

The FEEDBACK corrects the movement…

So focus on the feedback and the movement will work.

Focusing on feedback is not something golfers are taught, so I understand that it is new to you. Just remember that <u>getting the feel right makes the movement right</u>.

Again, Focus on Feel First.

OK, back to the regularly scheduled content...

It was not until I developed Bio-Visual Focus that I understood the real value of this drill. Until then, I hadn't broken the drill down to see what made it work so well.

In Golf Swing Control, I broke down the backswing, the transition, and the downswing into parts. Doing this, I made a mistake that I believe may have slowed the progress of many golfers. Breaking the swing down into parts, even though those parts are more about movement rather than positions, still moved golfers into a more conscious, technique based mindset, which goes against how the mind and body work together during a golf swing.

This swing drill works for most swing styles with slight modification. If you use the more common weight shift, follow this drill as it is written. If you stay on your left side during the backswing (Gary Edwin style or Stack and Tilt style) as some of my students prefer, the difference is that instead of *weighting* the right leg, you will use the backswing to "set" or "pressure" the right leg muscles while maintaining a majority of your weight under your left side. If you have questions about this style of swing and how to apply this drill, email me and I will explain further.

This swing drill takes the place of the broken down golf swing from Golf Swing Control. I do this because a dynamic drill frees the mind from falling into the "technique based thinking" trap. It is also a much simpler explanation while still giving you all of the important feel points so you can repeat this drill exactly for your fastest swing development.

This drill also gives you the **best feel** for how impact will actually feel in the hands, and how the backswing should feel in the arms, legs and core.

If you practice this drill, all you have left besides a good setup is getting the transition right.

Without a good setup, this drill will do you more harm than good.

Start by setting up to the ball using the setup routine – there is a free video from www.golfswingcontrol.com or www.biovisualfocus.com. Just go to either site and sign up for the free videos.

Next – without moving the arms at all – turn your hands so that the club shaft points along the target line and is parallel to the ground. The handle end of the club should be pointing down the target line. Your hands should be in the same location as they started (this is very important). The toe of the club should be pointing up. In this position, the wrists are preset for the backswing.

At this point I want you to notice the position of your right elbow (if you're right handed). It should be tucked in, pointed at and touching the body. The left thumb is pointing away from the target.

I also want you to notice the base of the palm of your right hand as it sits on the left thumb. Again, the connection between your right palm and left thumb must be solid. This point where the hands join is the final power point of the swing. Although the fingers control the club and allow the wrists to move freely, this point is where the power is delivered from the body to the golf club. Once you feel this connection, it will be the point of focus for the hands position throughout the swing.

The preset position is where your hands and right elbow should be as they pass over the hitting area just before impact during the downswing. This is called the preset drill because you are presetting the impact position.

Now, keeping the club pointing straight back along the target line, make the backswing by pushing the club straight back along the target line. <u>Keep the weight felt under the feet under the right arch as you make the backswing</u>. To avoid a reverse pivot, make sure you are not adding weight to the left foot as you make the backswing.

The club shaft should keep pointing down the target line. As your body turns and your arms rise, the shaft of the club (and your right thumb) should continue to point straight up until it moves over your shoulder. At the top, depending on how flexible you are, the shaft of the club and your left thumb will either be pointing straight up or toward the target.

The club position at the top is important because allowing the shaft (or your left thumb) to slant behind you during the backswing will cause the hips to get out of place and rotate back toward the target. In the golf swing, something as simple as turning the wrists during the backswing will throw the hips out of position because the body will compensate to stay in balance. As your body turns, the club will find the proper position without turning the wrists because you automatically balance the club as you balance your body by monitoring the weight felt under your feet.

You should check your position at the top of the backswing in a mirror when you first start using this exercise. The upper body and head should be balanced directly above the inside edge of the right knee and the arch of the right foot with your chest pointing away from the target.

If it looks like you are leaning the upper body away from the target past the right knee, it means you were moving the club around your body rather than simply pushing it straight back away from the target. Moving the club around the body causes the right hip to turn and start moving back toward the target as stated before.

The left knee should naturally move in toward the right knee during the backswing. If the left knee kicks out toward the golf ball it is also a sign that you are moving the club around your body rather than pushing it straight back from the target.

Make sure the groove in the base of your right palm stays well connected to the left thumb during the backswing.

As you make your backswing, your right shoulder should naturally move directly behind you and your left shoulder should move under your chin as your body turns to make the backswing. This is one of the checkpoints that I carry over from Golf Swing Control. Your chest will face away from the target when the backswing is complete.

Many golfers complain that they just can't get the transition right. When I watch their swing I notice that they are often not finishing the backswing. If the backswing isn't complete, the hips may not be in the proper position to make the transition. As a checkpoint, looking at the ball at the top of the backswing, you should see your target side shoulder under your chin, turned behind the ball. Once you see this and feel the coil, there is one more small detail that will start your transition naturally. I'll get to it, but for now, watch the video.

Here is the drill. Nick Faldo demonstrates it. Take the time to notice the details I have mentioned so far that are not mentioned in the video.

https://www.youtube.com/watch?v=a6QtMgkK6zI

Or look up Faldo Pump Drill on Youtube.

Now here's the secret and my twist to the drill that really makes the backswing build more power.

I want you to get back into the setup position again with the club turned as before but this time, *I'm adding a slight change that will make a huge difference*.

Once again make the backswing, and as you do, feel the muscles along the inside of the right thigh as you push the club back for your backswing, but this time:

Push slightly down toward your right foot with the *palms* of both of your hands.

You should feel as if you are almost over emphasizing the wrist set. Push just enough to feel the muscles in the right inner thigh "set" in place. You don't want to move your body out of its best position. This should lock the right knee into a proper flexed position by the time your hands pass that leg. This move prevents a slide and is where you really build and store power. It also makes the downswing almost automatic.

The rest of the backswing should feel as if you are trying to push the palms of both hands against a curved rail that is guiding your club to the top of your backswing.

NOTE: Pushing with the palms of the hands guarantees proper extension of your arms during the backswing without over extending or pulling your upper body out of its best position.

You should feel a difference between the first backswing (which is probably your normal backswing) and the second backswing (with the leg set). During the second backswing, once the right leg muscles set, the rest of the backswing is like stretching a big rubber band located within your body core.

Again, keep the weight felt in the feet under the right arch. The left thumb should always be pointing either away from the target or straight up. Make sure the palm of the right hand stays connected to the left thumb.

As you make your backswing, your left shoulder should move under your chin as your body turns to make the backswing.

As a check, the right elbow should stay connected to the body until the hands get past the right leg. From that point the right elbow should always point toward the right hip and be bent at a right angle once your chest has turned away from the target.

Once you see your shoulder under your chin, your chest is turned away from the target, and the body has given what you feel is a good amount of resistance against that right leg...

There is one more very elusive detail that will make the downswing just about automatic.

The first time I experienced what I'm about to explain to you, I was in a Zone. Every shot was well struck. Every swing felt like it was in slow motion, but the most memorable part was that I saw my hands go through impact for every shot.

I had no idea of how it was happening but I knew I had discovered a very important part of the golf swing process.

This is the tiny little detail I have chased for 30 years and found again by accident when I sprained my left ankle to the point where I could not apply any weight or torque to it during the golf swing.

I was coaching a college golf team and the students wanted me to play along with them even with the bad ankle. After about 30 minutes of experimentation, I found that this weight movement allowed me to play without hurting my ankle, added 20 yards to my drive, and prevented my only occasional ugly shot, a nasty pull hook. Although I have never seen this kind of weight shift advocated, I would not go back to a traditional weight shift. If you've seen the Golf Swing Control Videos, you've seen how much head movement I had. The head movement protected my damaged back. With this new weight movement, I was able to swing with very little head movement and no back damage.

There was only one problem…

I couldn't pin down what I was doing that made the swing work so well before another injury sidelined me for yet another year.

So once again after I was able to heal, it was back to the drawing board. I knew what this new transition felt like but now that my left ankle was fine, I went back to my old tricks. I could no longer see my hands coming through impact, and my shots were less than stellar. At times, they were just bad. I was so close and yet so far away but I knew one thing…

I did everything right when I did this drill.

So what was it? What was I missing that I did during the drill on the practice range that I didn't do on the golf course?

After countless hours on the range plus many more hours studying the best Tour Professional golf swings, I thought I had it. I went out the next day and put on a demonstration of ball striking that amazed even me. It has been consistent ever since.

Here's the little detail the best I can describe it.

- You have to have a perfect setup.
- During the backswing the back knee has to stay in place.

As you finish your backswing using this drill, your target side shoulder will come under your chin and AS THAT HAPPENS, slowly force the arms up just a little more until the away side hip gets to a point where it feels like it's getting pulled apart just a little at the very outside point of the hip. There is a little stretch right there at the outside of the hip that when released, will set the downswing into motion.

For a while this little cue was elusive. Sometimes I could do it and other times I could not. I finally nailed down the detail that makes it work. My habit has always been to allow my head to drift over my right foot. I did it to protect my back, but once I realized what was happening I realized that I didn't need to move my head.

Once I stopped allowing my head to move over to the right during the backswing, I found that automatic downswing again. At the top of my backswing my head is behind the ball but inside of the right foot. My weight is under the inside of the right foot as well, but it feels like I am leaning a little toward the target because of the angle between the right foot and my head, even though I am not.

My secret to getting and keeping my head in place is to get a picture of the position of my head relative to my right foot once I am set up. As I make my backswing, my left shoulder comes under my chin, but stays inside of my line of sight to my right foot. The shoulder should get to the edge of your line of sight to the right foot and you should be turned behind the ball at the same time as you feel the stretch on the outside of the right hip.

Yeah, it's rather specific:

- Weight under right arch
- Shoulder under chin
- Turned behind the ball so you can see the ball with your left eye

- You can see your right foot with your right eye
- Feel the tiny stretch in the right hip

These little details make it very easy to stop your head from drifting and make the downswing more automatic. If you <u>don't</u> know where your head is relative to a fixed point (your right foot) you will not notice if your head moves. It's a tricky position but once you feel and see it, you'll be able to repeat it.

Two Triangles

To give you another mental picture, there are two triangles that must be right for your best golf. You probably know about the triangle between your elbows and your hands. Once that triangle is set, it shouldn't change shape.

The second triangle is experienced at the top of the backswing. The triangle is between the golf ball, your right foot and your target side shoulder. At the top of the backswing you should see the target side shoulder between the golf ball and the right foot.

As you near the top of the backswing, you will see the triangle form and start to feel a small stretch at your right hip. As you feel the stretch at the outside of your right hip, you can slowly bring your arms to a stop and the lower body should release to start the transition.

What happens is that the stretch (provided the right knee doesn't straighten) will send the right leg into motion to start the downswing as soon as the stretch is released. While this stretch and release is happening, I make an effort to keep the target side shoulder under my chin for a second longer so that the body starts the downswing properly. Releasing that shoulder too early can cause your upper body to turn out rather turn down and through the ball.

Ultimately, that little stretch and release is how the lower body starts the downswing before the upper body without the need for thought or any other movement to start the downswing.

Because the right leg starts in before the upper body can "jump off-sides" your weight also stays over the right leg just as it did for me when I injured my ankle and...

It is very easy to see the hands come through impact.

The weight transfers down and into the back of the golf ball adding "snap" and distance to the shot. Best of all this all happens before your brain can get involved and screw it up.

GRF – Ground Reaction Force

What I didn't know at the time I was developing this new backswing and transition was that this new weight shift makes efficient use of the principle of Ground Reaction Force (GRF).

What does the Ground Reaction Force do?

When you shift your weight to the target side foot in a traditional manner, you move your weight and power laterally and some of it ends up past the ball before impact.

But when you start the downswing keeping the weight behind the ball it feels as if you are pushing the right leg directly into the ground during the downswing. This ground push seems to build up the weight on the back leg while it is still coiled. Newton's law states that there is an opposite reaction from the ground, which is the Ground Reaction Force. The GRF acts to increase the release of stored power, multiplying the club acceleration during the downswing.

But there's more power to be found during the downswing...

The weight building up under the ball of the target side foot just before impact is where the stopping of the left side creates the whip effect of passing energy up through the body to the arms and hands. Because this whip effect happens just after the hands pass over the golf ball, the whip effect adds further acceleration to the club head as your wrists unhinge through the hitting area. This timing is how pros make the golf swing look easy while the golf ball takes off like a shot out of a gun. The whole "whip affect" is created by timing your weight movement properly at impact.

Chase the ball to the finish.

As you strike the ball, your last thought should be one of "chasing" the ball down the line with your hands as the ball leaves the clubface. This visual thought adds to your accuracy by preventing you from pulling the arms off line too soon.

This drill works for all clubs, including the Driver and you can hit balls using it. As a matter of fact, I used it on the golf course during a Play Ability Test when I just couldn't get my driver to be consistent. I actually hit every drive this way and didn't miss a fairway.

Once you get the hang of this drill, use it on the range mixed in with your regular golf swing. Switching back and forth will unify the drill with your golf swing and your new natural golf swing will be born. Switching back and forth is how I finally discovered the little hip stretch that made all of the difference in my shots.

This new golf swing is the one your body WANTS to make and once you are used to it, you will never need to change it again.

Shaping Shots using Balance

A perfectly straight shot with a big club is a fluke.
– Jack Nicklaus

Instead of adjusting your stance and grip every time you have to shape a shot, there is a much simpler method that doesn't require memorizing a million different combinations of stance and grip for each shot.

Using balance, the shot shape is created during the backswing.

It sounds hard to believe but with a little practice, you'll find this method very natural and super easy to remember. The greatest benefit is that you can't overcook a shot using only balance to shape it.

How does balance help you shape a shot?

Use <u>the same stance and grip for every shot</u>. The <u>only difference</u> is that *<u>during the backswing</u>*, you want to adjust where the weight is centered on the back foot to change the shot shape.

- For a straight shot the weight will be centered in the arch of the back foot at the top of the backswing.
- For a draw, the weight will be centered toward the heel of the back foot at the top of the backswing .
- For a fade, the weight is centered toward the toes of the back foot at the top of the backswing.

The key to making a properly balanced backswing and shaping shots is **moving during the backswing <u>at a pace slow enough</u>** that *you* can monitor AND adjust where the weight is moving underneath your feet.

Monitoring your weight during the backswing also sets the pace for your swing. This simple act keeps you from swinging too fast even when the pressure is mounting.

<u>Always start the stance with the weight in the arches.</u> Golfers have a tendency to want to start the stance with the weight in the heel or toes. Starting with the weight under the heels or toes is an out of balance stance that will kill the shot.

Everything else about the swing is the same except for where you move the weight to during the backswing.

How does it work?

Remember when I told you that balancing the body also balances the golf club? The placement of the weight during the backswing automatically adjusts the plane of the golf club to make the intended shot.

Moving the weight toward the toes of the back foot during the backswing creates a more upright backswing which results in a slightly out to in swing that results in a fade.

Moving the weight toward the heel during the backswing lays the club off and creates a plane that will result in a draw.

No matter what part of the back foot you move the weight to, always keep the weight under the <u>inside half</u> of the foot so the body doesn't go into auto-balance mode.

There is only one small change I have had to use for a few students. If for some reason, the fade isn't working, open the shoulders a little at setup.

Yes, it really IS this simple. Your best bet is to go to the range and hit some shots this way and see what happens.

Once you've come this far, you should be hitting the ball well, be confident in your golf swing and be ready for the real fun stuff.

The Mental Game – The Fun Stuff

It takes hundreds of good golf shots to gain confidence, but only one bad one to lose it. – Jack Nicklaus

"They" say that 90% of golf is mental. I say it's all mental.

At this point your mental game has already surpassed most golfers' mental games without once addressing your mental game.

How?

Remember when I said to get better results you have to work on the processes that create the results? That's what you have been doing.

During the setup routine you are required to do many tasks which require a delicate mental interaction between the conscious and subconscious. For example, when you look away and move your feet while feeling for the balance in your arches, you are using the process of active awareness. Your subconscious is making the adjustments to balance, but your conscious is letting you know when you are there. The two minds are already working together!

Also, when you look downrange while setting your feet, you have to keep a visual picture of where the ball is located to figure out how far to move each foot during this process. This visual picture jump–starts the visualization process for the actual golf swing.

This is important because what you have learned so far flies in the face of conventional swing and mental coaching practices. The results you have seen should tell you that conventional swing "wisdom" is flawed.

Any swing coach will tell you that a swing change takes at least 6 months or more. I've met more than a few golfers who have quit professional golf because the prospect of changing their swing and wasting 6 months or more doing it seemed like a total waste of time. The frustration alone drove them out of playing professionally.

Using active awareness properly, a golfer can make a swing change and use it smoothly the next day. It works because active awareness is a combination of the physical and mental games working together. Instead of changing technique, you change the mental/physical process that creates the technique and the swing adjusts automatically. (I will demonstrate this in a few minutes.)

Think about it: What *consistent* results has traditional golf swing or mental game coaching actually produced over the last 20 years?

Look at professional golf today. Today's golf professionals have the best technology for equipment, fitness and instruction. You would think that someone could figure out this one stupid little glitch all golfers have in common.

Yet, no golfer dominates the PGA tour; even those at the top struggle with this stupid little glitch. Tiger at his best had to grind it out now and then.

Now look back a few years to Nicklaus, Hogan, and Palmer. They didn't have all of the technology. They played with equipment today's golfer wouldn't dream of using, yet they didn't struggle the way today's golfers do from day to day.

What's the difference?

The golfers of the 60's and 70's didn't have mental coaches. Mental coaching started gaining popularity in the 80's.

In the 60's and 70's golf instruction wasn't super technical. Instructors didn't teach swing theory like they do today. Golfers found what worked for them and stuck to it.

So I ask, has the technology helped or... Has the expansion of golf instruction made things more confusing?

Knowing all of this, I decided to study golfers who didn't struggle with this glitch much on the golf course to see if I could find some insight for a simpler, more effective mental game centered more on execution of the golf shot.

After studying many of the great golfers, I decided on Hogan and Nicklaus because they each had elements of their routines that when combined, create a mental routine that just hasn't been seen to date.

Hogan had two secrets.

Hogan knew if he moved in dynamic balance during the golf swing he would make more consistent contact with fewer mistakes on the golf course.

Hogan also watched for his hands to pass through impact before the club dropped below parallel during the downswing. If he saw his hands in that position, and he was moving in dynamic balance, he knew he couldn't miss the shot. (This was the true purpose of his pump drill.)

Between these two secrets, Ben Hogan was one of the most consistent golfers of all time, despite playing for years in constant severe pain from a near death auto accident. If you watch his golf swing over the years he was winning, it was basically the same but day to day it was a little different. That didn't change his ball striking prowess because his balance and imagery were what made the swing work.

Nicklaus had one secret.

Nicklaus started the mental coaching revolution with one paragraph in his book, "Golf My Way" where he mentions seeing a picture of the ball going to the target during the pre-shot routine.

Amazingly, the mental coaching community completely disregarded the next sentence; the <u>most important part of the routine</u>: Nicklaus said he then saw a movie of <u>himself making the kind of golf swing</u> that would create the shot he saw in his mind.

The picture of the ball going to the target is a future conscious thought that can hurt you. Nicklaus's movie of him making his golf swing was a present subconscious thought that pre-programmed his body to make the shot. The part the mental coaching community ignored was the one piece of Nicklaus's routine that created much of his consistency and success.

So, when you read or hear that "you should focus on the target (landing area) during your golf swing", that's how this misleading advice came about. Unfortunately, that coaching is not only wrong, but it will lead to a real confusing time trying to reprogram your mind later when you realize the truth.

The purpose of the mental game...

To build an effective mental game and not get lost in all of the fancy distractions of mental training, you first need to realize the purpose of the mental side of golf.

As I said before, the plan for each shot is made in the conscious mind, but the conscious cannot guide the body movement of the golf swing, so the plan must be passed to the subconscious to implement the plan so your body's muscles receive the details for the next golf swing. While the subconscious is communicating the required golf swing to the body muscles, it cannot be interrupted if your golf swing is to work its best. That's the heart of the mental game and it really is that simple.

Most mental mistakes are a result of golfers getting stuck in their conscious mind. The rest of this book will show you how to prevent getting stuck and easily crossover to the subconscious mind whenever you need to on the golf course.

There is another layer to the mental game. There should be an overall plan for each round of golf depending on your goals. If you are in competition and you have to make up 5 shots to have a chance at the lead, you will play more aggressively than the golfer in the lead. In the lead, you play more conservatively and take advantage of any opportunity to add to your lead. This is all conscious stuff that happens between shots. Don't be fooled, **the mental process that happens <u>during the shot</u> is what makes or breaks a golfer's round of golf.**

There is a time to think about each part of the mental game and a time to let each part go. The letting go is the hardest part because it means the conscious mind must be quiet; not something it is used to doing.

The golf game goes sideways when the subconscious gets stepped on by the conscious. So if you are in the middle of the fairway on a perfect lie, you may not focus as much on the shot, until the shot gets ugly. When that happens, instead of focus, a subconscious state, your mind usually goes into a state of panic, which is a conscious state, which then can snowball into the "Frankenround" unless you realize what is happening.

The next few chapters will show you how to prevent and if needed, stop the Frankenround in its tracks.

What About Muscle Memory?

This is a game of misses. The guy who misses the best is going to win. – Ben Hogan

First of all, muscles don't have memory. All memory is in the brain. That said, there is a memory process for muscle movement. There are two parts to it. If you practice properly, you <u>can</u> make the golf swing almost automatic.

The first part of muscle memory happens whenever you learn a new movement. Memory is processed through the subconscious mind, usually in the form of pictures. If I ask you to remember something, you'll be able to recall it when you see some kind of image in your mind relating to it. I can remember faces but not names because faces are visual and the printed word is more difficult to picture.

Before learning a new movement such as the golf swing, you must first decide you want to do it. That decision happens consciously. That decision is intent. If you already know how to do something, your intent tells the subconscious to "upload" the program from memory and run it.

If you are performing a new task, the subconscious has to create a new program, which has to happen with the help of the conscious mind. This is the learning process. The conscious can't control movement, so information has to be passed from the conscious to the subconscious, which has to interpret the new information, convert the ideas into a form the muscles can use, pass it to the muscles and wait for conscious feedback to see if what happened was what the conscious intended. If not, conscious instructions are adjusted based on new information and the process starts over.

The constant passing of information between the conscious and subconscious makes the new task awkward. (Think about the process of learning to drive a car.) This back and forth checking of information repeats until the conscious is happy with the program the subconscious runs. That's when the task starts happening more smoothly. After that, practice consists of running the program and making small adjustments based on occasional conscious feedback. Once the process becomes habit, like driving, you can eat a burger, talk on the phone and drive at the same time with little thought.

The learning process is where actual memory for the new movement is created. There is a second process that makes repetition much easier. It is called myelination and it happens in the brain every time a neuron is fired.

To break it down, every time the subconscious sends out a "program" it sends electric pulses down all of the neurons needed to activate the muscles for the movement. Every time a neuron is fired, it is wrapped with stuff called myelin, which improves the neuron's ability to fire. The more the neuron is fired, the better it fires. A well myelinated neuron sends clearer signals to the muscles so the muscles make more accurate movements.

Here's the catch. There are many neurons for every muscle and the most myelinated neurons usually get the bid to carry the message to the muscles. If you myelinate the wrong neurons by grooving incorrect movement, you have to work harder to myelinate the right neurons to get the right movement locked in. That is why adjusting and "fixing" certain movements that you may have learned to do improperly is so difficult. While you are myelinating new neurons, old, myelinated neurons are still trying to hijack the job. This is also why habits are hard to break.

The good news is that when you train new neurons and ignore old neurons, eventually the new neurons take over and the old ones go back to "normal" size. Retraining the neurons usually takes 21 days of perfect practice. That is to say, every movement needs to be as close to the same as possible. Otherwise a larger group of neurons is myelinated and the messages to the muscles aren't as precise, which means your golf swing still creates some bad shots.

OK, now in English...

Whenever you make a move, the neurons that pass the message are boosted a little. If the next time, you make a similar move, but not exactly the same, different neurons are boosted. If in practice, every golf swing is slightly different, you will have a wide variety of neurons over time that are equally boosted, but the wide variety means that too many neurons are getting the message so it is up to the subconscious program alone to make your best golf swing. In other words, the program has to do all of the work and your golf swing may or may not work well depending on how much your conscious thoughts get in the way.

BUT if you can make the EXACT same movement every time, the same neurons are boosted and after a while, those neurons fire as soon as they know the program is coming. Because of the complication of the golf swing, the boosted neurons don't completely take over, but they make the job of the subconscious program much easier to implement.

This is what is happening when you walk. Your neuron network takes most of the job. If I ask you to walk and focus on where the weight is felt as each foot strikes the ground, rolls across the ground and again where you push off, you would consciously have to ask for feedback from the subconscious program. It might be a little awkward at first, but you can see the subconscious images of the weight felt under your feet as you walk.

You will also notice that each foot is a little different. If I ask you to walk, making sure the weight is felt only in certain places, such as the middle of each heel, the ball of the foot behind the big toe, and then from the middle of the ball of the foot as you push off, you could do it. It will be awkward because you will be correcting your existing walking program. In the process of learning the new walk, you will also be working to over-ride the older boosted neurons.

If you practice walking with this new weight feel pattern, you will eventually make it habit. But if you forget to practice, you will slip into your old way of walking as the original boosted neurons take over.

Back to the golf swing...

Can you make the exact golf swing every time?

You probably think it's almost impossible with all of the complications involved but...

There IS a way to make every golf swing so close to the same that the field of boosted neurons is narrowed and they do help the subconscious program.

How?

If you move in dynamic balance during your golf swing, you always move on the same path.

> **There is only <u>one</u> dynamically balanced swing path for each golfer**.

But there is an endless number of unbalanced paths.

This is the <u>mental advantage</u> of taking the time to make sure you move in dynamic balance every time you swing a golf club.

When you move in dynamic balance, you boost the same group of neurons that will eventually make the swing automatic.

Using Active Awareness to monitor your weight and make sure you move along a balanced path as felt in your feet, not only insures you make perfect contact, but it also boosts the neurons to create <u>true</u> muscle memory.

BUT REMEMBER: With either Muscle Memory or the subconscious swing program – Both methods require communication between your brain and your body.

Swing Tempo

A side effect of monitoring weight movement during your golf swing is that you cannot feel AND CONTROL your weight movement if you swing too fast, <u>so you will need to be moving at a slow enough pace to make sure you can feel AND CONTROL the weight</u> during the golf swing. **This is how you create the proper tempo for your golf swing.**

Active Awareness is the mental side of movement that helps build Muscle Memory, or in actuality, Neuron Memory for your golf swing while also improving the subconscious program for it. Improving your Active Awareness makes it easy to mentally crossover from a conscious state to a subconscious state.

How Active Awareness Works

"You must work very hard to become a natural golfer."
-Gary Player

If I ask you to take a walk, you probably wouldn't think at all about your feet. But if I ask you to tell me in detail where you feel the weight pressure along the bottoms as you walk, you would walk a little slower as you focus on what is really happening during your walk. If I ask you to do so without looking at your feet, you will have to use Active Awareness to be able to tell me what is happening.

What really happens during the Active Awareness process?

I ask you to tell me certain information about your body that you can only feel. Your conscious asks the subconscious for the information. The subconscious tells the conscious that it has to experience it to be sure, so you perform the activity. The subconscious gets the feedback and feeds it to the conscious in a form the conscious mind can translate and communicate; usually picture form.

Try the exercise and see what I mean. Take a walk. As you walk, figure out where the weight pressure is felt in terms of middle, inside or outside half of the bottom of each foot. Figure it out for:

- The heel as you land.
- The bottom of your foot as you roll across your foot.
- The front of your foot as you push off.

Do so by walking without looking at your feet. Each foot will feel a little different.

Did you see some kind of image in your mind representing the weight pressure felt under your feet as you walked?

If not, do the exercise with your eyes closed.

Doing this exercise shows you that your subconscious communicates with your conscious mind using pictures. This is important because when you see the pictures the subconscious creates to communicate with the conscious, you can see what is happening in your body and you are seeing it happen LIVE, in the present moment.

What is also important is that doing this exercise uses your conscious and subconscious together. You would not have taken the walk if you did not first have an intention command from your conscious mind.

Now if I asked you to make sure that when you walk, you land in the middle of the heel, move to the ball of the foot behind the big toe, and then push off from the middle of the front of the foot, you can do it.

Try it now, again, without looking at your feet as you walk.

This time your conscious intention command is different. During this exercise your conscious takes the image of how you normally walk from the first exercise and, based on the new instructions, it adjusts that picture. Your conscious then tells your subconscious to run the new program. Your subconscious runs the new program, and you probably walk a little slower to accomplish the goal, but you do it. You are slower because you are in the learning phase of the new movement. If you practice properly for 21 days, the new way of walking will become habit.

The walking exercise shows that your body movement can be adjusted <u>immediately</u> using Active Awareness. Your golf swing works the same way as this walking exercise and can be adjusted just as quickly.

It is important to note that in changing how you walk I DID NOT ask you to focus on your walking <u>form</u>.

If I were to try teaching you how to walk properly <u>based on form</u> it would go something like this...

Start by stepping off with either foot. You want to lift your knee 35 degrees and lean forward 17 degrees at the same time. As you lean forward, roll across the back foot and bend your knee 22 degrees. As soon as the stepping foot touches the ground on the heel, push off with the back foot and pick the foot up bringing the knee to 72 degrees until the foot passes the now planted front foot. Once the back foot passes the planted foot, allow the knee to extend to 30 degrees in preparation to land that foot...

And a good walking tip (golf tips?) would be something like: *Don't forget to roll your knee outward slightly when stepping past the planted foot...*

How long would it take you to learn to walk that way? Forever! Can you imagine seeing magazines dedicated to teaching you better walking form? Yet, <u>that is STILL how golf is taught during mainstream instruction!!!</u>

After seeing how trying to learn based on form looks for walking, does it make sense to focus on golf swing <u>form</u> to fix your golf game?

Instead of trying to explain form, I focused on the process or internal <u>function</u> that creates your movement in relation to the force of gravity. You used gravity feel points that your brain and whole body reacted to and your walking form improved right away. How much practice did it take?

In contrast to Active Awareness (of body <u>function</u>), the emphasis in traditional golf mind training is to separate your conscious and subconscious minds and keep them separated.

Their intention is to quiet your conscious mind so your subconscious will just take over and make your golf swing without conscious input. <u>But your conscious and subconscious minds don't work separately.</u> Your conscious tells your subconscious what to do, what memories to bring up or what programs to run for the body through the use of conscious intentions. Your conscious is the boss so it will want to stick around to make sure your subconscious has loaded the correct program. Telling your conscious to take a hike is like telling a child to go to bed early... There will be protests! Is it any wonder modern mental training really doesn't help much?

Professional golfers rely heavily on their routines to keep their conscious mind from getting involved during the shot. Mainstream mental coaches teach golfers to trust their routines, their judgment, and their golf swing <u>But what do you do when, despite all of the trust, things aren't working</u>?

How long can you trust your routines and your golf swing while watching the golf ball go everywhere but where you intend?

DOUBT – The big swing killer.

Sometimes it takes only one mistake to start the landslide in your mind that leads to a day of grinding on the golf course. For many veterans, they can go throughout the round without worry, knowing they will just write the day off and come back tomorrow and things will be different. Usually things are different and the professional golfer lives to fight another day.

Sometimes though, things don't improve from day to day and you start doubting your golf swing or blaming something else for your lousy golf game. Doubt is made up of conscious thoughts that hang around, create more doubt and quickly kill your golf game.

Depending on the situation, there is always a breaking point.

When things get too bad, golfers will often resort to a complete overhaul; a new golf swing, a new mental coach, or a new caddy... All to get rid of nagging doubts. The process can take years for a golfer to recover and some never do.

It doesn't have to be this way, but to stop this trend in your mental game; you have to know why it happens and get out in front of it. The secret is in understanding how the mind functions during movement.

Practice

Golfers are taught in mainstream mental instruction that hitting 1000's of golf balls builds muscle memory, as if the repetition alone causes the mind to remember the movement.

But there is one glaring element missing from that picture...

You are building the muscles that make the swing, but the muscles can't act consistently or accurately without a clear subconscious program to fire the neurons that activate the muscles.

PGA golfers have good subconscious programs to hit the quality of shots you see them hit. When a PGA Tour golfer starts hitting stray shots, it means the subconscious program isn't getting to the muscles.

The reason that the program isn't getting to the muscles is usually because a balance override in the subconscious has hijacked the muscles, or the conscious intention has been blurred by doubt or another bad conscious thought.

Even muscle (neuron) memory won't help if the subconscious doesn't know what program to send to the muscles.

This communications breakdown happens because the conscious and subconscious have been trained to stay apart and aren't trained to work together during the golf swing.

Imagine if you were doing some delicate operation that required lots of focus and right in the middle of it, something crashed through the ceiling in the room. There is no way to stay focused unless you practiced with that kind of distraction. For a golfer using traditional mental methods, when the conscious steps in during a shot, the result is very similar to something crashing through the ceiling.

On the other side of the spectrum, using active awareness, your conscious and subconscious are trained to work together, the same way they function normally. During the pre-shot routine Active Awareness insures that the correct swing program is loaded. The process also lets your conscious know that your subconscious needs to get the program through to the muscles so your conscious can see the results it wants.

The result is that your conscious mind, once trained, helps to protect your brain/body communication rather than interrupting it unknowingly.

Using Active Awareness during your routines and during your backswing also keeps your conscious quiet, but still a part of the swing process. Just as the conscious checks the feedback during the learning phase, it does so when using active awareness, but the conscious doesn't have to step into the process because it has been there with the subconscious every step of the way and it <u>truly</u> trusts the process.

Active awareness converts your doubting conscious mind that was constantly criticizing your mistakes into a conscious mind that is giving "thumbs up" signs or positive reinforcement during your golf swing. (Your conscious becomes Chuck Norris)

Active awareness is important for consistency for two reasons:

Mentally, Active Awareness builds <u>real</u> trust in your golf swing, whereas when your two minds are kept separate, the conscious is merely holding back its doubt until it sees something go wrong.

Also, using Active Awareness during the backswing, you insure that you:

- Stay in balance.
- Follow the one true swing path for your body build.
- Swing at a proper tempo,
- And continue to build neuron memory with every golf swing.

So, both mentally and physically, Active Awareness helps your golf game with less stress and less practice.

Why Routines Are Important

You swing your best when you have the fewest things to think about. – Bobby Jones

Each shot starts with a conscious plan or intention. If you're lucky, the shot you need "just comes to you." It means you're in the Zone, but there is still a conscious intention to load a subconscious program. In the Zone, the conscious intention seems automatic and you barely notice it.

Whenever you are on the golf course, you start every shot routine consciously but you hit your best shots when the conscious quiets down after initiating the plan so the subconscious can do its best work. A consistent process for moving from a conscious state to a subconscious state is what mental coaches have been looking for since mental coaching started.

In the Zone, the transition to the subconscious mind happens without effort. It's not something a golfer wants to analyze if he's in the Zone, which is why nobody has figured it out until now. The rest of the time, a golfer has to find a way to calm his conscious mind. For most people, the idea of quieting the chatterbox in their head seems impossible.

This is where routines come into play.

In golf, the purpose of a routine is to control the conscious thoughts that interrupt subconscious communication with the body. Every part of a routine must have a purpose, either to eliminate a judgment such as deciding how to grip the club (a conscious process) or to eliminate doubt, as doubt will quickly snowball and create more doubt. Each part of a routine must have a purpose or it must go.

What makes the golf routine difficult to perform is the conflict with your every day routines. Think about your shower routine. You probably have a process you go through; when you shampoo your hair, or wash your face; how you soap up and in what order. You probably don't second guess how you are washing yourself the way you may second guess your golf stance. The shower routine allows your mind to think about other things. Some of my best ideas have come to me either in the shower or while driving.

In everyday life, your routines allow you to think about something else while performing the routine, but in golf, the idea is to not think, which is direct conflict with every other routine you perform daily..

So how does using Active Awareness during your pre-shot routine change this?

Let me use an everyday example to demonstrate how your mind works where you probably don't realize you are in a zone. It starts with a simple question.

Which would you rather do; read a book or see the movie based on the book?

Most would rather see the movie because reading the book is more like work. Here's why: When reading a book, the written word has to be converted in your mind to a form the subconscious can use. When watching a movie, the information streams straight into your subconscious because it is already in picture form; the form preferred by the subconscious.

Think about what your conscious does during a good movie. Doesn't it quiet down and watch along with your subconscious? Now think about how you think about other things during a normal daily routine. Aren't those thoughts mostly visual?

The idea of Active Awareness is to place your mind in a "visual" mode so your conscious can relax. When the shot plan has been passed to your subconscious mind, your conscious should then quiet down and watch the plan unfold in very much the same way you would rather watch a movie than read a book.

Being aware of what your conscious and subconscious minds are doing allows you to also know when you are in a zone and WHY without suddenly losing the zone. With awareness you are in control of the zone rather than spending your rounds hoping to find yourself in the zone and then hoping it will last the whole round.

During the pre-shot routine given earlier in this book, you are required to picture certain things. (**Remember:** The feel points are converted into pictures when stored into memory.) This is where your subconscious starts working. A good routine keeps adding pictures to the pre-shot routine until just before the golf swing starts. Once your original conscious plan has all been converted to the proper pictures, your golf swing has been moved into your subconscious mind.

Active Awareness allows your mind to crossover from the conscious state needed to plan the shot into the subconscious state needed to successfully complete the shot while keeping both minds aligned toward the same goal.

Active Awareness During The Shot

If you did the walking exercise earlier, you could feel and see in your mind how the weight pressure was felt under your feet as you walked. The visualization is a product of asking your subconscious for the information your nerves are sending from your feet to your brain.

For Active Awareness to work its best, the pictures used during the pre-shot routine must be directly related to something your body can feel. Those are the only pictures your body movement can respond to accurately.

Now the $64,000 question: Is there a body related feel that relates to the landing zone target?

I ask because modern mental coaching tells golfers to focus on the landing target. This is important because you can keep that picture in your mind as the mental coaches tell you to do, but that picture creates a conflict in the subconscious because there is nothing body related or feel related to connect to in the mind. Without an internal connection, the subconscious will either disregard the picture or be distracted by it. Unfortunately, without a picture the subconscious can relate to body feel, your muscles don't get clear instructions for the golf swing.

Again, any time you move your body, the subconscious puts up a program that works in a visual mode. The easiest way to prove this is to have someone blindfold you in a room full of various obstacles and spin you around. When you try to move around the room, you will have to reach out to protect yourself from hidden objects. The moment you touch something, your mind will fill in the picture of the object, and then the picture of the rest of the room. Once you have the pictures, you know how and where you can safely move in the room.

The pictures that you have to create while blindfolded are the ones your subconscious relies on normally except you don't realize you are using those pictures. Before your subconscious will allow you to move, it has to have all of the information.

Now try hitting a golf ball with your eyes closed. It isn't easy. I want you to first try focusing on the target as you swing. Don't try too much as you might hurt yourself while digging up ground.

Now try again, but this time instead of worrying about hitting the ball, just try to see the picture that your mind is struggling to see as you make your golf swing. Your mind will try to see the golf ball whether your eyes are open or closed. You will only hit the golf ball when your mind can see an image of the golf ball. That image is the anchor for the movement program your subconscious is running.

If you are keeping a different image in your mind while your subconscious is trying to focus on the golf ball, it's a subconscious conflict between the two images that can diminish your ability to hit great shots. That was demonstrated in the first part of the exercise.

What should you picture?

Good question!

- Your subconscious needs to focus on the golf ball to hit it, even with your eyes open.
- The golf shot is decided by the path of the club as well as the direction your club face is pointed at impact.

Wouldn't it make sense to convert your shot picture into a picture of your golf club coming through impact the proper way to create the shot you want?

That way, you would focus on the ball the way your subconscious wants to, but you would also have a picture in mind relative to the target your conscious is worried about. It's the best of both worlds.

Remember during the walking exercise when you replaced your normal walking picture with the new one and your body responded?

Getting the right impact picture allows your subconscious mind to make tiny little corrections to your movement during the downswing to further increase the accuracy of your shots.

BUT REMEMBER - It can't happen unless you are moving in dynamic balance so that your auto-balance mechanism doesn't ditch the swing program.

So balance is the first part of the equation, timing is the second part, and then once you are moving in properly timed balance, correcting the impact picture finishes the job to create some of the most amazing golf shots you'll ever hit.

Creating the Right Impact Picture

Golf is deceptively simple and endlessly complicated; it satisfies the soul and frustrates the intellect. It is at the same time rewarding and maddening – and it is without a doubt the greatest game mankind has ever invented.– Arnold Palmer

Hogan had two secrets. One was balance and the second one was his picture of impact. Balance creates consistency and the impact picture, and as long as the body movement is well timed, creates super accuracy.

There are some caveats before I reveal the optimum impact picture for best results.

- You must be moving in balance. Without balance, you have no access to the subconscious pictures you will use.
- Your body sequence must be correct. The lower body always leads the downswing. (That little hip stretch from the swing drill makes this happen)
- Keep the weight felt in the bottoms of your feet behind the golf ball until impact. This is part of the

swing drill that keeps you from getting ahead of the golf ball.

So what was Hogan's picture at impact?

Hogan wanted to see his hands pass over the golf ball with the club still parallel to the ground and the club shaft pointing toward the target just before impact.

Hogan wanted to see the same picture just before impact that you see over the golf ball at the start of the preset drill. He knew that if he was balanced with the right body sequence, when he saw his mental picture actually happen over the ball, the shot would be good. This is why Hogan used the pump drill so much in his teachings. The pump drill brought his hands and body to the correct place to see his "secret image" come to life.

This is probably the most consistent shot-making lesson a golfer can learn. Performed properly, <u>it works every time</u>.

Right now you're probably thinking I'm nuts, but Ive done this so many times with near perfect results that I know I have found the pinnacle of the golf swing. There is no greater feeling in golf than to know you can see this image come to life and to witness the flawless shots that are a result of this final piece of the puzzle.

Before you rush out and try it, this is not easy to do. Start with your short clubs. Get a wedge and hit pitches looking to see this picture.

Make sure you are in balance with your lower body leading every shot.

Your subconscious mind does the rest. If you have loaded the picture in your mind and everything else is working, your mind will create the correct result. Once you start seeing the club coming through impact with short irons, move up until you can see it with your driver.

Again, <u>proper weight shift is crucial to make this happen</u>. If you allow too much weight pressure under your front foot too soon, you won't see the hands pass through before impact. This is where the little hip stretch at the top of the backswing becomes crucial too. Without it, you won't be able to see the picture actually happen.

This works for the sand as well. If everything is working right, you can also hit a flop shot off of a tight lie if you see this picture materialize during the shot. It's that good.

Shot Pictures

In order to visualize any shot and create agreement between the conscious and subconscious, you need to know how the club head and golf ball must meet at impact to make any type of shot. Here are the basics:

The golf ball starts its journey on the path your club was moving at impact. For a right hander, if your club is moving:

- Inside the target line to outside the target line through impact – The ball will start to the right.
- Down the target line – The ball will start on target. (Actually, inside the line, then down the line and back inside the line. The club can only stay on line for a distance equal to the distance between your hip pointer bones.)
- Outside the target line to inside the target line – The ball will start to the left.

The golf ball will finish in a direction decided by the direction the club face is pointing at impact. For a right hander:

- If the club face is open at impact (pointing right), the ball will curve to the right – a fade or slice.
- If the club is closed (pointing left), the ball will curve to the left – a draw or hook.
- To make the shot higher – Approach the ball on a steeper plane.
- To make the ball go lower – Approach the ball on a lower, more sweeping plane.

To make combinations:

- An inside to out swing with an open face is a push-slice.
- An out to in club path with a closed face makes a pull-hook.

- An inside to out path with a closed face is a roping hook.
- If you swing outside to in with an open face, the ball will start left and slice into the next county.

Not only can you make your intended impact picture knowing this information, but you can analyze what your swing is doing during bad shots based on where your shots are going.

Fades and draws can be made using balance alone or a combination of balance and impact picture.

Regardless of the type of shot you wish to hit, you must always start your golf swing from a properly balanced stance.

I can't emphasize this point enough. The biggest mistake golfers make is to start their swing from an unbalanced stance. Even using balance to shape shots, you must always start in a neutral, balanced stance.

To review making shots using balance:

- To fade a shot using balance, at the top of the backswing feel for the weight to be more toward the toes (inside half) of the back foot. This will steepen the backswing and produce a slight out to in path that will create a gentle fade.
- To draw a shot, feel for the weight to be under the heel (inside half) of the back foot. This will lower the club plane and create a gentle draw.

ONLY once you get comfortable using balance to shape shots, you can start looking for your intended picture to happen at impact.

Important: Shots cannot be shaped using your impact picture by itself. You will ALWAYS need to have the balance component to shape shots. Balance adjustment to shape shots works with or without adding the impact picture to the mix.

Again, the impact picture IS NOT a substitute for using balance feel to shape shots. It is only added to the use of balance for better accuracy.

Also: Adding the impact picture only works if you are at the point where you actually see your hands pass over the ball before impact. If you're not there yet, keep practicing with shorter clubs until you start seeing the hands just before impact.

- The impact picture for a fade is where the club is parallel to the ground and the shaft is pointing slightly out to in across the target line as the club passes over the ball just before impact.
- The draw picture will have the shaft pointing slightly in to out across the target line as the club passes over the ball just before impact.

If these pictures are clear and you are swinging in balance, your subconscious will take care of following the intended picture and the intended golf shot will actually happen.

The Zone/Body Connection

The mind messes up more shots than the body.
– Tommy Bolt

There is a physical connection between your body and the Zone. It is your body's parasympathetic nervous system. The opposite system, the sympathetic nervous system, is the fight or flight response your body experiences in an emergency.

There is a great likelihood that you are signaling your fight or flight sympathetic nervous system to act on a daily basis with one simple action you don't even realize you are doing. Performing this action on the golf course will certainly stop you from entering the Zone.

What is this perilous action that is causing your body to stress out unknowingly?

The simple action is your breathing. Without thinking about it, many people breathe through their mouth every day, and because mouth breathing signals the sympathetic nervous system, it is creating all sorts of hidden stress, inflammation, and more.

Nasal breathing, on the other hand, has been proven to calm the mind and body because it is connected to the parasympathetic nervous system.

Why do we breathe through our mouth rather than the nose? It seems easier. Close your mouth and breathe exclusively through your nose and you'll see what I mean. If you're a mouth breather, you've probably been doing it so long that it has become habit. As a result, your body and mind will have a difficult time trying to relearn to breathe through your nose.

Why breathe through the nose? Here is a list of known benefits:

- Enhanced mental clarity and focus.
- Optimized energy levels.
- Enhanced elimination of body toxins through the lymphatic system.
- Better blood acid/alkaline, which increases resistance to various bacteria which can make you sick.
- Nasal breathing actually massages the heart, relaxing it.

There are many more benefits but there is one benefit that should especially interest you as a golfer:

The ZONE <u>cannot</u> be reached unless you are breathing through your nose.

If you want to experience the full pinnacle of golf during a golf shot, you have to be in a subconscious state. Nasal breathing is a necessary part of the formula.

Nasal breathing isn't easy. It is something you will need to relearn; yes, you were a nasal breather when you were born, probably right up until you had your first stuffy nose.

I'm not writing a book on nasal breathing, but there is a very good one out there. It's called, Body, Mind, and Sport, by Dr.

John Douillard. I highly recommend that you get this book and read it to enhance your chances of reaching the Zone by relearning how to breathe efficiently through your nose.

The Pre-shot Routine

The pre-shot routine is where the mental and physical sides of golf come together. This is where you take the conscious plan and move it into the subconscious for execution by the body. It is a simple step by step process that puts together all of the elements discussed in this book.

Step One: Start by making sure you are breathing through your nose.

Decide what shot you want to hit. This will be your conscious intention. It sounds easy at first, but this step also involves eliminating as much risk as possible from the shot.

The plan must start from where you wish the ball to finish. Do you know how far the ball will roll when it lands? Will the ball roll into trouble? There is nothing worse than a perfectly executed shot that lands and runs into a hazard.

You have to start by knowing what the ball will do when it lands. A draw will roll a lot farther than a fade.

What shot do you plan on hitting after this one? You want to leave yourself so that your next shot gives you the best possibility for a birdie without causing a bogie or worse.

Take the time to consider all of these possibilities and you will have less bad luck on the golf course.

Step Two: Once you have decided on your shot, you need to visualize the shot to see how it may be affected by the elements or any obstructions.

Step Three: Just like Jack Nicklaus used to do, see the shot as a line in the air from the landing spot back to where the ball lies now. If you've watched golf commentary on TV you've probably seen how they trace shots through the air.

I want you to take this one step further and take the line coming back from the target through the ball and up to the top of the backswing.

Step Four: Make a practice swing following the backswing line you just visualized to feel where the weight in your feet needs to be during the swing for the shot. Use the preset drill if needed to program the feel in the feet and see the impact picture. (I highly advise making this part of your routine.)

Step Five: Visualize the club shaft coming through impact in a manner that will create the shot shape you want. The handle should follow the line you traced back through the ball up to the top of the visualized backswing. Again, It helps to use the preset drill or Hogan's pump drill to physically see the impact picture you will need.

Step Six: Set up to the ball.

Step Seven: Let go of the target picture, Make sure you have loaded your weight picture, the picture of the golf ball relative to your body movement during the backswing and your impact picture as discussed in the previous chapter. After some practice these pictures will become a movie in your mind.

Step Eight: Make your golf swing.

Once this step by step routine becomes habit, you will have conquered most of the demons plaguing your golf game.

Why Does This ALWAYS Happen To Me?

Of all the hazards, fear is the worst. – Sam Snead

Sooner or later this thought crosses your mind. You feel like the golf gods are out to get you. Once this thought shows up, if you don't know how to handle it or thoughts like it, **you are toast**.

You are going to hit some bad shots and you will get your share of unlucky bounces. When something bad happens it's easy to think that it only happens to you. Each member of your foursome is probably thinking the same thing about their own game.

Conscious thoughts are impossible to just block out. Like a crowd around a public murder scene, they just hang around to see what's happening. Left unchecked, those stray thoughts hanging around will ruin your round of golf. Here's the secret to get started dispersing the "conscious thought" crowd... Face the fact that:

Bad bounces happen to ALL golfers!

Watch the PGA Tour looking to see just the BAD shots and you'll be surprised at how many there actually are. The pros hit it into the trees all of the time too. They just don't show it much on TV.

So you're not so special when it comes to bad luck. If you think you have more bad luck than the next golfer, THAT very thought is the problem.

What I'm saying here is that you may be causing many of your own problems. The explanation of why gets a little involved, but the first step is to realize that YOU are the one creating the thoughts that are sabotaging your golf game.

Step One – They are *your* thoughts. (I'll prove this to you in a few minutes.) You create them and you CAN... no, MUST deal with them if you intend on playing great golf. (Just like any treatment program, the first step is owning the problem and admitting you need help.)

Step Two – Dealing with bad thoughts is a lot easier than you think. You start by catching them before they do any harm.

Thoughts are constantly running through your mind: So much that you only notice the important thoughts.

When you ask yourself a question like, "Why does this always happen to me?" do you fully realize that you asked yourself the question?

This question is very sneaky because it has two meanings. On the surface you are wondering why you are having bad luck, but deep inside, you have given up because you're "doomed" to continue having the same bad luck you always have. By asking this question to yourself you have assumed the worst is going to happen, so your mind will probably comply with the request.

Yeah... It's twisted the way your mind works, isn't it?

There is a lot going on up there in that brain of yours, all at the same time. As you are reading this, you may be also thinking about the thoughts you have on the golf course that hurt you. It's possible to think on two or more planes at the same time. I find myself coming up with some of my best ideas while I am reading a book. There I go again...

The trick is to start catching these thoughts as you have them and really look at them. Give your thoughts categories and rate them good or bad. Ask yourself if you really need to be thinking those thoughts. If you say "no", the thoughts should start going away.

And now I must take you on a journey down the rabbit hole to understand this whole conscious – subconscious thing...

The Rabbit Hole

For this game you need, above all things, to be in a tranquil frame of mind. – Harry Vardon

Most of our thoughts (the ones we are worried about that concern your golf game) are either conscious or subconscious…

Conscious thoughts are either about the past or the future. They are either good or bad for you. Many times <u>just realizing that a thought exists and that it is a bad thought</u> will be enough to let it go.

If you are thinking about the last shot or the next shot, they are conscious thoughts. Thinking about the outcome or score is also a conscious thought.

Subconscious thoughts aren't actually cognitive thoughts but rather picture streams or videos about some action you are doing or may have done. There is a interesting crossover when it comes to the past. If you are thinking ABOUT a past event, it is conscious, but if you are simply recalling the event as a video, the video is subconscious…Unless you react emotionally to the video in your mind, at which point the thoughts are conscious again.

For the majority of your time, you are either reviewing a past event, thinking about the future or both. If you happen to be in the present in your mind, your subconscious is in charge. The present is where action takes place and the subconscious handles action. There are no conscious thoughts in the present and the present is where you want to be when you are hitting a golf ball.

Here's the real crazy thing:

One second into the past or future is still the past or future, but you can close that gap down between the past and future to a nanosecond either way.

So if the present is less than a nanosecond, does it even exist?

Actually, it's a trick question. Man invented the concept of time because we have memories. Time exists only in our minds; in our memories. (Don't forget; this IS the rabbit hole)

You can't actually change the past and you never know for sure if you affected the future because you can't go there to see what it would have been without a specific action.

Even though they exist in your mind, the past and the future don't exist physically. You can't touch either one. You exist in the present.

Let me be more specific: Physically, you exist in the present. Your <u>mind</u> can be in the past or future, but when it is, you are squandering the present moment because you are not focused on it.

This is why I say that YOU create those thoughts and you can control those thoughts. Those thoughts can ONLY come from YOUR mind because that is where the past and future exist.

Past and future thoughts steal your existence by taking your mind away from the place you actually exist: the present.

What is the present?

Simply put, the present is the task at hand or whatever you are *doing* at the very moment.

Here's the catch: You can't perform in the present without information from the past to make sure your plan for the future works. You have to plan each shot (a future event during the planning phase) based on knowledge gained from past play. When you are planning, the act of planning is a present thing, but if you get caught up in your past or future thoughts, you pop out of the present. Otherwise, you are only in the present when you are in the act of swinging the golf club and hitting the golf ball.

Those bad thoughts that mess up your shot creep into your mind during the planning phase, so it's important to be aware of bad thoughts during that time. It's important to make sure you don't get tied up by past or future thoughts during planning. It's a very delicate balance. You can watch your past or future thoughts... But don't get wrapped up in them!

How do you know if you are getting caught up in past or future thoughts?

Your emotions are an indicator of where your mind is at any time. In the present, there is only action, so there are no emotions. On the other hand, if you are in the planning phase and you find yourself getting emotional about a past or future thought, you have been hijacked by the thought. This includes being happy about a thought as well as being upset.

About negative thoughts

When you see water, do you say, "Don't hit it in the water"? It's a bad thought. What picture comes to mind when you say that? The water, of course!

Your brain uses pictures to create body movements, and to do so it turns conscious commands into pictures.

The process of converting conscious thoughts into subconscious pictures cannot deal with negative thoughts. "Not the water" becomes a picture of water. Whatever you say NOT to do becomes a positive command. You don't realize it unless you become aware of the pictures that guide your movements.

When you catch yourself using negative conscious commands, try to see the picture that is created by the command. If the picture is bad, you need to stop and reword that command. Instead of "not the lake" you should focus on a spot in the fairway. "Don't slice" should turn into, "approach the ball on an inside out path" or another image that gets you on the correct swing path.

Ultimately, to steer your thoughts back to the present, they need to relate to the task at hand. If not, those thoughts will create pictures that disagree with the present pictures your mind uses to create whatever action you need. That disagreement will dilute or corrupt the mental pictures and hurt that movement.

Once again, (I realize I am beating a dead horse here, but this is the biggest argument I get.) I go back to the question of focusing either on the landing zone or on the golf ball. The golf ball is part of the task at hand because you are hitting it _now_. The landing zone is where the ball _will land_ if you hit it properly, which is in the near future.

Focusing on the landing target is a tricky situation. If you focus on the landing target as part of your pre-shot routine, the landing target can be a subconscious thought, but once you pull the trigger and start the golf swing, the landing target becomes a distraction because your subconscious will focus at the ball. This is why there is always such a heated argument about where to focus during the golf swing. The key words and the ones that matter are, "during the golf swing", because that is when the glitch occurs.

In contrast, a picture of the club moving through the impact zone is subconscious because it is related directly to the task at hand, hitting the ball. If you focus on the landing target picture, that distraction will dilute the program being sent to the muscles for your shot, which can cause a mis-hit.

How to deal with bad thoughts

First, you must be aware of your thoughts. Start by monitoring your "behind the scene" thoughts on a daily basis. The more you do this, the more you will realize how cluttered things are in your mind. That clutter can really do some damage on the golf course.

When the boss is bugging you about something you find unimportant and you start thinking about what a fool he is in your mind, catch those thoughts.

When a friend does something bad for them, but absolutely predictable and you say something like, "Why does he always do that?" catch that thought. With practice, you will find yourself constantly monitoring your thoughts. That is the idea.

Take some time to notice the emotions you have that are connected to those thoughts. Those emotions will hurt your performance on the golf course.

Next, realize that some thoughts just won't go away. Yes, that sucks but there is a way to deal with them.

To start with, every bad thought (or good thought) has a "trigger" that brings it out of your memory. There are events, situations or places that deep in your mind have been connected to bad things and for whatever reason; those connections got stuck in your mind. Now every time you encounter one of those triggers, the thought connected with that trigger comes up.

For example, I have triggers for funny lines that I sometimes blurt out. They just fit certain situations, and when I'm in one of those situations, the thoughts just pop up. Under normal situations, I can't think of those one-liners. But as soon as the trigger happens, out they come.

Whenever you have a persistent thought you can't get rid of, and you are aware of the thought, you have to identify the trigger that is connected with it. <u>Once you have the thought and the trigger, you can change the thought</u>.

About 15 years ago, my wife and I were driving when we saw a car flip over on the Savannah River Bridge and almost go over the wall. Everyone was ok, or so I thought. After that day, whenever my wife would drive over a bridge, she would slow down, sometimes to a crawl. She had a fear that was triggered by the accident on the bridge. The bridge was the trigger.

After talking with her, I realized that she had a fear of drowning if her car went into the water. She didn't know what to do in such a situation, so her subconscious took measures to avoid the situation. I explained exactly how to escape a car if she went into the water and once she realized she would be Ok, she never had the issue again.

I was able to identify the fear because of the trigger. I was able to change the relationship of the thought with the trigger by adding new information to the thought. Once the new information was added, the thought no longer interfered with her driving.

To change a thought, you start with the trigger. The trigger helps to identify the fear or belief behind the thought. Once the reason for the thought is identified, the reason or fear can be removed with new information. The bad thought can then be replaced with a proper, positive, new thought. You may also need a new "reminder" trigger to bring up the new thought for that situation.

You can have fun with reminder triggers. In your daily routine, you will come across a thought you are working to replace with a good thought. As soon as the bad thought comes up, perform some action such as slapping your hand or something innocent like tapping a certain part of your head. The repetition of the action will remind you of the new thought. This is where the 21 days of repetition mantra comes into play. Eventually, you will replace the thought and you can drop the reminder trigger.

Why replace the thought? Why not just get rid of it?

Many times, to get rid of a thought, you would also have to remove the trigger. Removing the trigger may not be possible because many triggers are external events that are out of your control. In my wife's case, there was no way to prevent driving over bridges.

During a round of golf you need to do something a little different. You get to a hole with a drive over water. You may wonder if you will make it over the water. If you have the yardage to clear the water you can figure out what other clubs you can clear the water with. If you know you can clear the water with your 3 iron, your mind should let go of the thought of missing the drive so you can swing without that nasty thought ruining your drive.

When I have thoughts like this I tap my backside with the handle of my club. That's my trigger that I have a bad thought that I must rethink so I can refocus on my routine.

Whatever trigger you create is a wakeup call to get you back to focusing on turning your plan into the correct picture to make your shot.

If you go through your preshot routine and focus properly on the shot, conscious thoughts won't get to you.

How you describe a hole tells a lot about where you are focused. I was talking to a golfer the other day and he was describing one of the holes he didn't do well on in a recent tournament. He started with, "It's a tight dogleg with water on the left and OB on the right." The first word, "tight" says he has little chance of hitting the fairway. Then when he talks about the trouble, he was thinking about where his ball would land, and wouldn't you know it; it landed in trouble every day. In cases like this, your own description of the hole is the trigger. You should use the information to decide the best initial target to line up with. When you pick a target, you change your intentions from hitting into trouble to hitting to the target, a much better thought.

In my case, I might get to a hole and realize that I never do well on the hole. That thought is certain death, so my trigger is that I have a negative thought. I change the thought to, "Hey, treat this one like a driving range." Then I think, "What's my target and what's the shot here!" and that gets me into the shot routine and the thought goes away.

It goes like this:

1. Notice your conscious bad thought.
2. Identify the trigger.
3. Adjust and redirect your thought (To neutralize the effect of the trigger) to be presently focused and get back to your routine.
4. Let your routine work its magic.

If the thought comes up during the routine, do what the pros do: <u>back off, go through this process again, and start over</u>.

Your pre-shot routine should move you from the conscious thoughts needed to plan the shot into the subconscious pictures and feel needed to hit the shot. As long as the routine gets you properly focused in the present, the conscious mind will want to watch the golf shot happen rather than get involved.

"I just don't belong out there..."

"There is NO try... only DO there is..." Yoda

I've heard the words, "I just don't belong out there" from budding professional golfers too many times. It comes out just after an attempted qualifying round. This one thought has held back more talented golfers than any other conscious thought they may have had during a round of golf.

If you've already played in a mini-tour qualifier or maybe a regional US Open qualifier, you've witness some spectacular golf, usually from a mini-tour player or a past PGA Tour player. It's easy to look at them and believe you don't measure up.

You'll be surprised to know THEY probably have the same thoughts. They may see you hit a great shot and think that they just can't compete any more.

Tour Players don't break through and win until they have learned to deal with this thought.

How do you deal with it?

First you have to realize that you aren't alone. 80-90% of current PGA Tour players have this thought too! I know that doesn't make things any better but knowing that the other golfers you are competing with have the same thoughts means you are on equal ground. Get over this thought and you will have a leg up on them.

So how?

First, realize one very important fact: You are human, just like they are; which means you have the same capabilities as they do. You put your pants on one leg at a time.

I know that isn't comforting but remember you are dealing with a THOUGHT that YOU CREATED and all you have to do is let it go.

It all comes down to making a decision.

I don't ever think this disastrous thought because a long time ago I made the decision that if another human being could do something (that was within my body's possibility), than so could I! If I didn't know how, I knew I could learn.

That's why I never gave up on this book despite great opposition to my discoveries.

The fact is, I DON"T CARE what other people may be thinking about me. I KNOW WHO I AM, and I like who I am.

I say that because the thought you are dealing with is a thought you have projected onto other people. It's not that

YOU think you don't belong. It's that you think THEY think you don't belong.

That's not their thought... It's yours! You created it and they are probably NOT thinking it about you. When you tear this thought apart, doesn't it sound absurd?

LET IT GO. Believe in yourself.

Believing in yourself is a choice you have to make before you try something you might have doubts about.

NONE of my instruction would have ever made it on paper if I didn't make this very same decision when I first started my free golf newsletter online back in 1997.

I remember fretting for weeks about whether I would be laughed at or scorned for creating my golf newsletters, even though I had already seen incredible results from golfers using my methods. I went for a long walk on the beach and instead of getting caught up in my thoughts; I stepped outside my thoughts and analyzed what I was thinking. I realized that the only person that could really stop me was ME... and I decided to believe. The rest is history.

Now it's your turn. Instead of thinking how bad things might get, think about all of the positive events and accomplishments that have lead to you wanting to succeed at something you love. Don't let a silly thought stop you.

Replace that thought with the decision that you CAN do whatever you set your mind to do.

Getting in a little deeper...

When you believe that you don't belong, you DOUBT your abilities and WORRY about the FUTURE. These are all conscious thoughts that will prove this crazy thought to be true... If you let that happen.

But I am a Star Wars fan. My favorite phrase is from Yoda: "There is no try, only do there is."

If you are "trying" you have doubts (conscious thoughts that lead to failure), but when you merely "do" you are present. When you believe you can, then you can focus and just DO it, as Nike states.

Lastly, you are not competing against any other golfers when you play in a tournament unless you are playing match play. Otherwise it's between you and the golf course... And the golf course is the same for every player.

So if you feel you don't belong out there you have 2 choices.

Either give up golf because with that thought you have already failed.

Or choose to:

- Believe in yourself
- Just do it
- Play the course
- Remember that with these simple choices, you have the mental advantage over the field.

The Mental and Physical Aspects of Putting

Putts get real difficult the day they hand out the money. – Lee Trevino

Putting isn't much different from hitting a full shot when it comes to the mix of balance, feel, and visualization needed for mastery.

Reading the Putt

Reading putts is probably the most difficult part of putting. Sometimes you just see the putt, but most times you have to figure it out.

Start at the hole and try to imagine the ball rolling the last foot or two toward the hole. Try to see how the ball will break going into the hole. If you can see the line the ball will roll on going into the hole, you have a good chance of making the putt.

Next, check the same line from behind the hole to see if what you saw at the hole seems the same. If it does, look at the line from behind the ball.

If all three views of the last foot or two are in agreement, take the fall line into the hole and extend it out about 1/3 of the putt distance and use that point for your aiming spot.

Once you have your aiming spot, try to visualize the ball rolling the whole way to the cup. If what you see in your mind agrees with your aiming spot, line up and make the putt.

If what you see when you visualize the full roll to the cup doesn't agree, step back and try to visualize the full roll to find an aiming spot that you feel good about.

Sometimes the line looks like it goes one way from behind the cup and then another direction from behind the ball. If it's not a big break, putt the ball at the cup. If the break looks bigger, check the putt from both sides and look at the overall slant of the green.

You will probably find that most of your putts will follow the 1/3 rule coming back along the fall line of the putt for your aim point.

Making the Putt

As in every other part of golf, you must be in balance for two reasons:

- If you are out of balance, the body will reroute muscles from making the putt to getting you back in balance and you will not make a good stroke on the ball.

- If you are not in balance, your subconscious mind will not allow you see the picture needed for the putt and reading the putt will be more difficult.

In the putting setup, balance comes from allowing the arms to hang down and moving foot to foot while looking away from the ball the same way you do it during the shot setup routine. Feeling the balance in the feet during the setup applies to putting just as it applies to hitting a shot.

In your setup position, your eyes should be directly over the ball. You can check it by setting up and then dropping another ball from your eye to see where it lands relative to the putt line. If your eyes are outside the line, you'll have a tendency to pull your putts. If your eyes are inside the line you will push your putts.

My secret for putting lights-out is simple. For right handed putters, make sure you set up in a way that your right elbow naturally contacts the front of your body and make sure it stays there throughout the putt. This applies for the short game as well. To be more exact, going back to the preset drill; when you turn your wrists to bring the club parallel to the ground, your elbow (away from the target) should touch your body. That is the same point where your elbow should connect to your body for putting and short game shots.

What's so special about attaching the right elbow to the body at setup?

Well, I have to say that for a long time, I was a horrible putter. I tried everything to figure out a consistent putting style, but the only thing that was consistent was when I practiced with only my right hand. I realized one day that putting one handed, I always had my elbow attached to my body. That's when awareness of what was really happening kicked in.

With my elbow attached to my body, I was amazed at how accurate my feel for distance was. My putts were also on line more often.

Most golf coaches teach their students to rock the shoulders to make a putt. Rocking the shoulders places the burden of feeling the distance on the tiny fast twitch shoulder muscles which cannot make the small adjustments needed when changing from an uphill to a downhill putt. That kind of control comes from core muscles because they routinely have to balance and control the upper and lower halves of the body during movement.

When your elbow is attached to your body, the core muscles become the distance control muscles, which is why your distance control will improve putting this way. Just about every one of my students who has adopted this method has seen better distance control and accuracy with their putting.

But there's more…

My putting grip and stroke are also important for accuracy.

I use a standard reverse overlap putting grip (It's the same as the club grip except the target side index finger is on top of the lower hand). I use my left index finger to start the back stroke while initially keeping the hands still until the stroke starts. I simply apply pressure using my left hand index finger to the right hand. The pressure starts the putter head moving back along the line (still without moving the hands until the putter pulls them naturally). The result makes the putter act like a pendulum where the shaft of the putter always points to your body center.

Doing it this way:

- Keeps the wrists from turning to open or close the putter face.
- On fast greens allows a minimum back stroke so you don't hit the putt too hard.

For the forward stroke I do something else unique.

With a reverse overlap putting grip, the left thumb contacts the base of the right palm by the thumb. I use this contact point as a mental reference. Instead of worrying about the putter head, I imagine that I am pushing the ball with the palm of my right hand specifically at that contact point between the hands.

Imagine that you were to just push the ball to the hole with the palm of your right hand. Ignore everything else and move just that contact point toward your target. You will be amazed.

To get the feel for how hard to stroke the putt, make your practice strokes feeling like you are pushing the ball with the palm of the away hand (both hands on the grip) while looking at the hole and visualizing the ball rolling toward the hole. You will feel the stroke in your core this way.

Hold your finish during the practice stroke until you see the imaginary ball fall into the hole.

Using this method, if your practice stroke is too hard or too soft, your visualization will reflect what you felt. Make another practice stroke until you feel like the imaginary ball is rolling the correct speed. When your practice stroke feels just right, step in for the putt.

There is one more detail to my putting routine that many golfers don't believe is possible...

Until they actually do it.

There is a very subtle mistake many golfers make without realizing it. Professional golfers spend lots of time working on eliminating this putting mistake. It is the mistake of moving the head to watch the ball roll as you stroke the putt. When you lift your head, even a little, your body moves out of position and the putter moves offline, throwing the putt off.

The cure for this seemingly innocent mistake is the mental "mind split' that makes for great putting.

Once you are set up and ready to make a putt, take one more look at your aim point and take a mental picture of the line to the hole. Keep that picture in the target side of your mind and focus on it while watching the ball and the putting stroke with the other eye, in my case, my right eye. When you stroke the ball you will keep your head down because you are putting the ball into the picture you already have stored in the target side of your mind. Since you have already visualized the ball rolling to the hole during your practice stroke, you're just recreating that visualization.

The mind doesn't know the difference between the real picture and the visualized picture. If the pictures are clear there is no urge to look up. That keeps your body from moving and affecting the putt.

One more thing: When turning your head to look at the putt line during your pre-shot routine, make sure you turn your head on your spinal axis. I've seen golfers pick their head up and turn their body to look at the putt line, which throws their body out of alignment relative to the putt.

There's a lot going on there, but once you incorporate these aspects of putting, you can 2-putt from anywhere and you'll roll in more one-putts than you ever have.

Short Game Short Cuts

There is an old saying: if a man comes home with sand in his cuffs and cockleburs in his pants, don't ask him what he shot. – Sam Snead

The short game isn't as difficult as many golfers make it out to be. The short game is actually a collection of a few techniques applied properly to affect ball flight. These chapters aren't long, so pay attention because each detail counts.

It is much easier to control your short game shots as long as you start with my first secret.

The biggest secret for the short game is to keep the right elbow (right handers) connected to the body during the shot (just like putting – the same location that the elbow connects to the body during the preset drill). So, during the set up, when you place the club and set your feet, move your body toward the ball until you feel the connection of that elbow to your body. This connection moves the responsibility for shot control away from the small fast twitch muscles in the arms and shoulders and to the core muscles which are better suited to gauge the swing force. I do this for any shot inside of 100 yards. The trick is simple: When you make your through swing, as your core turns toward the target, the body pushes the arms through the shot by pushing your right elbow where it contacts the body.

This same idea works for chipping. In addition, the closer I get to the green, the lower I grip on the club until I get to the bottom of the grip. This seems to give me more control as well. I find it also helps open your stance for a chip. The open body limits the backswing and increases torque felt in the core from the small turn made during the shot. After you have made the appropriate backswing for the chip, your forward body turn will push the right elbow through the shot. This keeps the hands ahead of the club head to help prevent the yips.

If you still get the "yips" while chipping, the cure is to use the target side hand as resistance to your right hand during the swing through the ball. It forces the hands to lead the club and forces the core to make the swing. So if you get the yips, try making your backswing using primarily the target side hand and then hold it there so you must force it through the shot with the other hand.

One last thing that helps especially closer around the green is mentally hitting the ball with the base of the palm of my away or right hand. Just like during putting, imagining that you are hitting the ball with your right palm makes the hands lead the shot and gives you good feeling for how hard to strike the shot for the proper distance.

No matter what shot you hit, including short shots and sand, the biggest trick is to watch for the hands to get through impact before the club. On a pitch or a sand shot, you want the club shaft to be parallel to the ground when the hands pass over the ball, just like a full shot.

Don't forget: On short shots, the core starts the downswing first.

For a flop shot, keep the elbow against the body and during the backswing, turn the hands so that the palm of the right hand is facing up. During the through swing, keep the right palm facing up and watch for the hands to get to the ball before the club drops below parallel to the ground.

Make sure the body is driving the arms through impact.

WARNING: If you are watching for the hands to get over the ball *with only an arms swing*, it will be very messy.

I'm sure it sounds hard to believe that the shot would work if your hands made it to the ball before the club dropped below parallel for such a delicate shot, but once you see it work, you'll be sold.

A pitch is the same as the flop except you don't turn the hands during the backswing. In practice, you can vary the amount you open the right hand and see how that affects the shot.

As far as weight distribution is concerned, for a pitch, stay centered; and for a chip, keep the weight under the target side foot.

Getting the Feel for the Swing

Just like putting, make your short game practice swings while looking at the target landing zone for your best distance feel.

Important: Pick a landing spot! If you look at the flag, you might land the shot by the flag and watch it run right by. Always keep in mind and plan for the roll after the ball lands.

Once you feel like the shot will fly to the landing zone, step up and make the golf swing you just programmed into your body.

REMEMBER: Watch for the impact picture during the real shot. I have found that splitting the mind for short shots works just as it does for putting.

Once you have the basics, you'll want to figure out how to make the ball go higher, lower and how to impart backspin. You'll have to experiment for yourself but I can give you some basics.

For chipping, approach the ball steeper during the downswing to make it pop up more and roll less and approach the ball on a shallower sweeping stroke to keep the ball low with more roll.

You can also curve your chips a little if for example you are chipping across a downhill and you want the ball to fight against rolling down the hill. An out to in stroke across the ball will give the ball cut spin. An in to out stroke will give the ball some draw spin.

You can also experiment with moving the ball back or forward in your stance when chipping to see how that affects the shot.

Have fun with your short game. Get out and practice. Try different things and you'll find some versatility to keep you interested in short game practice.

The Texas Wedge: The Texas wedge is using a putter from off the green, but there is a secret that reduces how much the higher grass on the collar affects the golf ball. The secret is to hit down and through the ball as you would a wedge. Doing so will cause the ball to jump up and roll across the top of the taller grass with less interference than if you tried to lift the ball by hitting up with the putter. This method takes some practice, so you will have to get out and work out the details for yourself to get a feel for how and how far the ball rolls when struck this way with a putter. Try it and you'll know why it was so popular for years.

One more rule of thumb to remember with your short game: The lower you can keep the shot (including rolling it instead of chipping) the better chance you have of making the shot. So, if you want to make a flop shot but a chip will get you there, always go with the lower shot as there is less room for error with the lower shot.

There's no reason to complicate the short game any further. These simple tricks plus some practice will have you playing short shots like a pro in no time.

Sand Made Simple

It's good sportsmanship to not pick up lost golf balls while they are still rolling. – Mark Twain

Sand isn't difficult. First you learn the basics, and then you get in a bunker and practice. Soon you will see why this chapter is so short.

When addressing a greenside sand shot, work the feet into the sand. Use the same setup routine except you need to hover the heel of the club above the ball. This will insure that you hit behind the ball and take sand.

The first trick for sand shots is the stance and the clubface are both open, which means a right hander's body is aligned left of the target while the clubface is aligned to the right of the target. The key is that <u>you swing back and through along the path you want the ball to take coming out of the sand</u>.

The right elbow stays connected to your body just as it should for all other short game shots.

The second trick is to keep the weight centered and during the backswing, turn the hands so the palm of the back hand is facing up, just like the flop shot. During the follow through, keep the palm up, use your body core to drive the swing, and watch for the hands to get to the ball while the club shaft is still parallel to the ground. To gauge distance out of the sand, turn the hands less open for longer bunker shots and more open for shorter bunker shots.

To make the shot go high, make a steeper approach into the ball. For a lower shot, make a lower, sweeping backswing.

The longer the shot, the longer the backswing and the less you turn your hands during the backswing.

AGAIN, the core starts the downswing for all of the short game shots.

Fairway bunkers

The best trick I know is to keep the lower body quiet. When you set up, pinch your knees together to help keep the lower body quiet during the swing. You'll make an out to in swing, so count on a fade and add one club to make up the distance loss.

You want to pick the ball clean in a fairway bunker, so a sweeping swing is the best bet. It also helps if you don't dig your feet into the sand when you set up.

Again, don't complicate sand. For pros, it's one of the easiest shots. This is an area where you can't practice enough. Once sand is your friend, it can be a great bail-out area when things look tricky.

Knowing you can always get up and down from sand builds confidence on the golf course.

Panic Time or Success?

A leading difficulty with the average player is that he totally misunderstands what is meant by concentration. He may think he is concentrating hard when he is merely worrying. – Bobby Jones

Why do golfers panic at the first sign of adversity?

I have seen the most talented golfers absolutely lose it and go into total brain lock over a single shot. Imagine if you did that in real life after a single mistake?

It doesn't make sense in real life and it doesn't make sense on the golf course. This book is not just a set of techniques to give you a better golf game...

This book is a manual to help you *calmly* maintain a great golf game.

If you look at the book as only a means to an end, you are only half way done with your journey. You <u>will</u> have those shots that make you scratch your head. Sometimes those shots will show up with money on the line. If you can calmly analyze any bad shot using the information you now possess, you can quickly find the root of the problem and fix it. You can stop the problem immediately after the shot and before you have a chance to hit another one like it so your game doesn't take a nose-dive.

If you aren't analyzing your shots yet, reread this book to discover how to figure out _why_ every shot acts a certain way so that when something goes sideways on the golf course, it isn't the start of a bad day.

Success is NOT a sudden quantum leap. If you study successful people in any field, you'll find that they don't have sudden success, but rather success that builds up slowly because of the small decisions and actions they make over time. It only LOOKS like they made a quantum leap because 80% of their progress is made during the last 20% of their work to get where they are.

In the case of golf, you probably know by now that just practicing will not make you successful. If you've been banging balls blindly at the range for years you can attest to what I'm saying. The lack of improvement with most practice is because "normal practice" usually happens with a disengaged mind. For long lasting success, the mind must be engaged in concert with the body to create consistent and deliberate intent for every shot.

The brain only records deliberate movement. Have you ever absent mindedly set your keys down and forgotten where you left them? When you hit balls absent mindedly, it's the same as losing your keys and a waste of valuable practice time.

Every shot you make in practice or on the golf course must be made with a purpose and a plan. You must use your pre-shot and setup routines every time. And most important, you must show up to practice consistently. 89% of success is showing up consistently.

Showing up for practice consistently is the difference between success and mediocrity. I ask golfers to spend 15 to 30 minutes each night before going to bed working on their setup and practicing slow swings using the swing drill in this book while feeling the weight movement under their feet. It's very easy to do, but only those who do this are practicing consistently. The routine is easy to do, but it is equally easy NOT to do. You won't notice right away when your game slowly deteriorates, but it <u>will</u> deteriorate if you don't do the drills every night.

Likewise, you won't notice right away that your game has suddenly improved if you do the drills every night. Success is sneaky. The drills may get a little boring and may not seem to be making a difference, but performing them <u>while paying attention to detail</u> on a daily basis makes small changes in your brain that slowly build up until one day, you're just hitting the ball perfectly, and you aren't sure why. On a chart, progress will look like a slow rise for a long period of time, but after a period that will make you second guess your actions, that curve will start rising faster and you will be playing amazing golf.

When you chart your results and see the curve of your improvement start to rise quickly and your golf game starts falling into place so much that you feel invincible... **Keep showing up every night to do the drills.** The moment you decide you don't need to practice every day is the start of the decline of your game.

Long term success is about "showing up" on a regular schedule and doing the little things that got you there.

Practice with the mind and body every night and hit every shot with deliberate purpose.

The Zone – Is it Really Difficult to Find?

Missing a short putt does not mean you have to hit your next drive out of bounds. – Henry Cotton

When a player is in the Zone, it's usually by accident. Once that player pops out of the zone, he isn't really sure how he got there or what made it stop.

Mental coaches are always touting how they can get a player in the Zone, but as I said before, with all of the methods out there, nobody is regularly playing in the Zone.

When I was working with players using my Bio-Visual Focus instruction, I had the privilege of working with Graham and Henry Boulton of Australia using their invention called the FocusBand. The FocusBand is worn on the head during play and picks up your brain waves. It can tell what state of mind you are in, including Mushin which is the Japanese term for the Zone. This apparatus is so accurate that when you blink, the face on the computer screen blinks!

When the students using the Focusband learned the Bio-Visual Focus pre-shot routine and used it properly, they always slipped into the Zone just before starting the backswing. *This was very cool.*

So how did it happen?

There are a number of prerequisites to being in the Zone. **The Zone can only happen when:**

1. The player sets up and swings in proper balance.
2. He or she is focused completely on the task at hand.
3. Their thoughts are visual/subconscious.
4. The golfer is breathing nasally.

Here's how it happens during Bio-Visual Focus.

As I said, every shot starts in the conscious mind with the plan. Once you decide the type of shot you want to hit, where and how you want it to land, step two is to see the actual shot in your mind. Visualization – The first step into a subconscious state. But that shot, no matter how you view it is in the future isn't it? This is where modern mental coaches have fallen short. They tell their players that the shot they see is the picture they should have in their mind when they set up.

So what is the answer? If you've been paying attention, you already know.

That shot must relate to the task at hand to be in the present. And... What is the task at hand?

The task at hand for your subconscious is the operation it is running at the time you are swinging the club and hitting your shot. So how does a golfer get into the present when he is holding onto a future thought? <u>He doesn't</u>! And that's why the Zone is so fleeting for golfers. They only find themselves in the Zone when they let go of the very picture that their mental coach told them to keep in mind.

How is this handled in Bio-Visual Focus?

In Bio-Visual Focus, you first take the shot picture and do just like Jack Nicklaus did; you see a movie of yourself making *the kind of swing* that would produce that shot.

But you're not done yet. Where is the subconscious focused? If you are paying attention, you'll know from trying to hit balls with your eyes shut that the subconscious is focused at the golf ball. Does the picture of you making your golf swing align your mind with the task at hand if your subconscious is focused at the golf ball? Almost, but there is one more step.

The last and most crucial step is to turn the picture of yourself making the swing to hit the shot into a picture that the subconscious can focus on WHILE it is focused on the golf ball.

I'm not going to let you off that easy! I already described what you should see earlier in this book. Your mission is to read through and find it. (Trust me, there is another reason for this)

Once you get to the pictures you will focus on at the ball, <u>you have to let the target picture go</u>. That is the hardest part. If you are focused visually at the ball with no other distracting thoughts, you are in the Zone. It is that simple. Again the only thing I can add is to be breathing nasally so you are tapped into the parasympathetic nervous system.

Getting there takes practice, but it's not voodoo or magic or even luck. The Zone is just about understanding where your mind must be focused and how it must be focused.

If you think about how the golf swing, the golf shot and the pre-shot routine are presented in this book, the whole goal is to do everything using the subconscious mind. Feeling your balance uses the subconscious mind. Monitoring the swing and the weight felt in the feet for swing timing uses the subconscious mind. The pre-shot routine moves your mind from a conscious state to a subconscious state. Doing all of these things even in practice helps you to find the Zone.

The Zone is where you are invincible. Now you know how to get there. You probably want to re-read this book and pay more attention to the details that help you get into the Zone.

K.I.S.S.

Golf is a science, the study of a lifetime, in which you can exhaust yourself but never your subject. – David Forgan

Well, I have certainly done that. When I started this journey, I never thought I'd spend thirty years figuring out this game. You certainly shouldn't have to take that long.

The results I am privileged to witness in just one or two sessions with a golfer prove the information in this book to be the simplest and easiest way to get your game to the highest level. I believe in the KISS principle; Keep It Short and Simple.

Given all of the complicated systems you'll see on the golf instruction market, you may have a hard time believing that a game so difficult could be so easy. That's why it took so long to figure out. It's also why most golf instructors scoff at my material and later ask what my real secret is for getting such fast results.

Don't fall for the hype. There are no deep secrets other than the fact that you need to use all of your brain alongside your body to make this game work. Once you start using this information, you will understand and the game of golf will become enjoyable.

Don't worry about your fellow golfers figuring out your secret. You can tell them and even show them, but the majority of golfers will go right back to complicating the game and adding to their frustration. I guess that's just human nature.

A word of warning: Other golfers, instructors and even mental coaches WILL work on convincing you that what you are doing won't work. I know this because more than a handful of my past students have been literally talked out of their golf games by these people... Even after they were seeing great success!

They do it because it is simple human nature. As a rule, golfers are convinced that this game _has_ to be complicated, so anyone who has found a simple way to play great golf MUST be doing something wrong.

Don't forget that your goal is to simplify, play your best golf, and enjoy the game. It is so much easier without the nightmares caused by technical instruction or conscious thought mental training.

The rule is simple. If you are getting the results, it's working. Don't forget where you came from. If the same stuff you were using before wasn't working, going back to it probably won't get you any better results.

Before you abandon this system, especially if you have already seen great results, call me and tell me what is happening. I may be able to "talk you off of the ledge" and get your game back on track.

Instead of getting tied up again with technical instruction, keep showing up and doing the simple drills that will consistently improve your game over time and you will enjoy a lifetime of great golf.

Drop me an email. I love hearing your feedback and answering your questions. tareed59@gmail.com.

So now what do you do? That's the next chapter.

Further Study

Many golfers reading this will want hands on training. My goal with live or video training is to get you to at least a +4 handicap. With that handicap, you can compete and win on just about any Tour.

There are two ways to get this training from me directly. The first is by video, online. That is the Bio-Visual Focus course at

www.biovisualfocus.com.

The videos on the website are as good as having me beside you... Provided that you pay attention to the details both in this book and on the videos. There are 11 lessons; each one adds a little more focus and accuracy to your golf game. There is no need to change your golf swing. If you follow the fundamentals I lay out in this book, you should already have an efficient, repeating, natural golf swing.

The videos will further explain how to use this information. Best of all, the membership is lifetime, so you can move along at your own pace. I do monitor your progress and open each lesson when you have satisfactorily completed the previous lesson because going too far too fast has had consequences in the past. I want to make sure you succeed.

The second way to get my teaching is in person. I live in a remote area and unfortunately the local golf course doesn't like me teaching there during the tourist season, so I have to pre-arrange and many times the answer is no if they are busy. As well, there is not a decent hotel near my community yet, so accommodations aren't real convenient. Also, I have retired from teaching full time as it is quite a drain on my personal time.

So instead, for the right student, I will teach concierge style. I will come to you and go through the training. This method works for me because I don't have to schlep around a bunch of equipment. The golfers I have worked with like that they can work in a familiar environment. I have also had golfers combine training with vacation, where I met them at the resort where they were playing. I'm flexible with location.

Remember, I'll teach you how to use your own built in computer and visualization machine so you have it on the golf course. And best of all, it's not cheating. Everyone who plays golf has the same marvelous built in computer equipment, except _you_ will know how to use yours any time you need it to eliminate any doubts about your golf game.

My fee if I feel you are ready for personal instruction is $1000 per day plus expenses and I am yours morning to night if you want to live and breathe this stuff. We can go over videos, talk theory, and play golf, it doesn't matter. After initial training, you'll have unlimited access to the Bio-Visual Focus video course to reinforce the training and make it stick. There is nowhere else in the world to get this training. So, if live training suits you better, give me a call at 239-227-7989.

So that's it. Either way, before you get lessons from me in person, please read through and use the information in this book. You will be surprised at your results from the book alone. Feel free to email me with questions. I also want to hear about your successes.

Hit'm well,

Tracy

62008384R00110

Made in the USA
Middletown, DE
17 January 2018